Spanish Painting

Spanish art began among the Cro-Magnons of 20,000 BC and
flourishes today with Salvador Dalí. In between, Spain made a
major contribution to European culture and was the home of
some of its greatest artists: El Greco, Velásquez, Goya.

In his examination of Spanish painting John Moffitt uses the
familiar art-historical designations of periods, but he underlines
the national within each of these styles and further points out
how Spain has been a more fertile ground for solitary genius
than for schools of painting. Exploring the character of Spanish
painting, he comes to an analysis of the Spaniard's mental
make-up. What emerges is a people of contradictions, conservative yet delighting in irreverences, aristocratic yet sensitive
to folk idioms. Above all, the keynote of the Spaniard and of
Spanish art is in the tense balance between the material and
the spiritual.

Front Cover: detail fromVelásquez *Las Meninas*
Back Cover: detail from Dalí *The Metamorphosis of Narcissus*

Spanish Painting

John F. Moffitt

Studio Vista/Dutton Pictureback

A J. C., maestra en generosidad y en intelectualidad,
a cuyo estímulo e inspiración se debió el impulso que
dió origen a este libro y a mis demás obras.

J. M.

Copyright 1973 in all countries of the
International Copyright Union
by John F.Moffitt
Published in Great Britain in 1973 by Studio Vista Publishers
Blue Star House, Highgate Hill, London N19
and in the United States of America by E.P.Dutton and Co., Inc.
201 Park Avenue South, New York, NY10003
Set in 10 pt Bodoni
Made and printed in Great Britain by
Richard Clay (The Chaucer Press), Ltd, Bungay, Suffolk

ISBN 0 289 70115 5 (paperback)
ISBN 0 289 70116 3 (hardback)

Contents

Introduction

It may be assumed that the arts of all countries within the mainstream of Occidental culture will, at a given moment, tend to approximate one another and fall within the pattern of the period. Accordingly, one will find within this brief survey of Spanish painting from its beginnings to its present state period designations – Romanesque, Gothic, Renaissance, Baroque, etc. – used in the sense that they are universally employed in the history of art. However, as the subject is specifically Spanish painting I have endeavoured to underline the unique national character as it shows through the successive period styles. It will be noted that in several cases Spanish tradition alters the larger period-sense to a degree that transfigures it. In this manner, it is hoped that the proper balance between the national and the international may be maintained in order that both may be appreciated.

The plan of this book concerns itself with two questions: 'What does Spanish painting evolve from and where did it go?'; and the more difficult one, 'What is the nature of the Spanish character as revealed in this painting and by what means is it specifically expressed?' In answering the second, I have tried, within this necessarily brief compass, to point out both formal and psychological motives which are recurrent enough to seem truly characteristic. I hope they constitute a credible case for the reader.

The Spaniard, it hardly needs stating, is quite a different sort of person from the Anglo-Saxon. The history of Spain and of its culture is a fascinating series of contradictions. For instance, on the one hand, an obsession with the sheer *material* quality of life is plain and yet, on the other, the Spaniard himself seems careless or disdainful of material objects and possessions. While he is ambitiously given to grandiose schemes and ideals, he is careless of their execution or ultimate realization. There is an innate aristocratic reserve in the Spaniard's makeup, yet there is a very strong democratic folk element in his culture which demands a pragmatic end for art and which is not congenial to lofty idealism. Spain is obviously an intensely religious country and most conservative and yet the withdrawn Spaniard delights in irreverences and satire. Spain is a land of the solitary individual; specifically, in the artistic sense, there is a dearth of 'schools' in the sense of followers of a particular master such as occur in Italian or French art. The historical nature of the harsh and divisive Spanish topography makes each region a hermetic entity and Everyman an island.

But, above all, it is the tense balance between the material and the spiritual which is the keynote of Spanish art. The expatriot Elena de La Souchère states that 'the Spaniard is gifted with a lively imagination. But *it is a visual imagination* nourished by the concrete and operating with difficulty in the abstract.' Nearly two thousand years ago a native of Córdoba, Seneca, enjoined his countrymen to 'set aside all ostentation and estimate the value of things by their uses, not by their embellishments . . . let us remember that all things are equally unimportant, presenting a different appearance on the outside, but equally empty within'.

In painting it will be found that its major interests are expressed in religious subjects, portraiture and still-life; characteristic of these genres is that they are all especially susceptible to a moral or analytic treatment – or both. Conversely, relatively ignored (or 'misunderstood') are landscape, mythology and the classical nude. For example, St Sebastian becomes an exercise in anatomy and ideal form for the Italian while the Spaniard decorously clothes him and concentrates his energies upon the painful nobility of martyrdom.

1 Beginnings: 20,000 BC to AD 200

The antiquity of the arts within the Iberian peninsula is undeniable. A comprehensive history of its painting encompasses nearly twenty millennia as the dawn of man, in Spain, was also the dawn of its painting. The first, surprisingly accomplished, flowerings of this venerable tradition are to be found within dark recesses of caves in the Northern and Eastern periphery of the peninsula; due to their placement, this art is sometimes known as rupestrian. Properly speaking, these works belong to the High Paleolithic period (or the later stages of the Stone Age) the greatest brilliance of which, as seen at Altamira, falls specifically within that period known as Magdalenian.

The peoples who created these brilliant masterpieces, tall and long-boned Cro-Magnons who displaced the squat Neanderthals, were hunters whose life centred about the dangers and mystique of the chase upon which they depended and which vital interests are so clearly and forcefully depicted in these spritely and spontaneous works. Of interest here is the thesis that this appears to be the first time in history in which one finds a division of labour, due to an economy of (occasional) abundance, which released some from purely food-gathering activities and thereby created a more or less specialized artist class.

These works seem to have served a magical, totemistic role – by ritualistically creating (and *ipso facto* 'capturing') the image and 'killing' it, the painter put the actual prey within the hunters' power. Certainly, this is not an example of 'art for art's sake': the often superimposed and usually compositionless imagery bears evidence to the contrary. The drawings were endowed, as it were, with a brief and functional 'psychic life' and once their immediate ends were attained they were 'not to be seen' any more. Hence the nature of the later additions which patently ignore the earlier works beneath. One must also note that the creation of the images in these dark and secluded caverns took place over many generations.

The actual materials employed are permanent colours derived from oxides and ochres finely ground. The powders would be stored in receptacles of bones, shells and even human skulls. The technique has been called 'impressionistic', and this is accurate inasmuch as it describes the brilliant capture of a fleeting illusion of life and movement. While these forms are to be seen throughout a wide Pyrenean region covering Southern France and Cantabrian Spain, perhaps the most impressive site is that of Altamira (Santander province), discovered quite by accident in the later nineteenth century and now faithfully recreated in all its vaulted splendour in the National Archaeological Museum, in Madrid.

The rupestrian tradition as later carried on in the Spanish Levant,

Reproduction of superimposed etchings and paintings from the Grand Salon of the cave of San Román de Candamo (Asturians). *in situ.*

in the Mesolithic or Middle Stone Age, underwent significant changes representing the very opposite of the Altamiran tradition and suggesting, by comparison, a certain aesthetic decline. These peoples of the South-East seem to have been more concerned with human activities than those of the North. Scenes of men pursuing animals and vice-versa become common and there is a clear differentiation between the sexes. The style is more cursive and sketchy.

Already in this early period one discerns a characteristic regionalization of styles due to the rugged and divisive nature of the Spanish topography, a tendency which is of cardinal importance in the development of Spanish art even in our own times.

The glimmerings of a specifically Spanish cultural admixture are to be seen in the Celto-Iberian synthesis: the Iberians, perhaps migrating from North Africa, were settled in the Peninsula by the sixteenth century, and the first Celtic (Indo-European) penetrations occur by the ninth, from the North. In general, the Celts occupied the centre and north of the peninsula, whereas the Iberians habited the coastal littoral where they developed a literate and complex society often given to luxury.

To the Greeks, ancient Spain was *Hesperia* (westerly land), whereas to the Carthaginians it was *Spania* (land of rabbits). It appears, also, that this 'westerly land' was the site of the Biblical Tarshish (Tartessos), the phantom 'Eldorado' of Antiquity, perhaps to be found in the Guadalquivir or Guadiana River estuaries. It is also thought that the name 'Spain' might be derived from the *Hispani*, an eastern Iberian tribe from the neighbourhood of ancient Massalia (Marseilles), who were defeated by the rampaging Celts and forced back into the Pyrenees. To the Augustan geographer Strabo it was *Iberia*, a term probably arising from a native term for 'river' as a main centre of Iberian culture was located in the fluvial valley we now know as the Ebro, near modern Barcelona.

Thus, in these early epochs, one notes the eclectic fusion, constant in Spanish culture, of the major traditions of the African, the Trans-Pyrenean and the ever-strong influence of the major Mediterranean cultures. The mixtures of the warlike, nordic, mobile, fair

Group of Archers preparing their Bows and Arrows and trying out some Shots.
Reproduction of rupestrian paintings in the 'Cueva del Civil', Barraneo de Valltorta,
Albocazar (Castellón de la Plana). *in situ.*

Celtic peoples (known as Gauls in France) with the wiry, slender, reddish-complected, non-Indo-European-speaking Iberian stock laid the foundations for the present Spanish race.

Of more lasting significance than the Carthaginian and Greek colonizations, confined to narrow and limited coastal regions for the most part, was that of the Romans. The Latins imposed upon Spain many things of lasting import: two hundred years of intermittent, but savage, warfare (more or less culminating with the defeat of Numantia in 133 BC) and then four hundred of the *Pax Romana*, the eventual basis for the common Castilian language, urbanization, the imperial concept of unity through centralization realized by the physical means of highways, bridges and aqueducts – some of which are still actively in use today – and its universal system of law.

The sobriety, veristic realism and stoic reticence of the Latin was found to be especially congenial to the nascent Spanish character; a first-century Roman visitor, Tragus Pompey, noted that the natives of Hispania were given to a life that was *dura omnibus et adstricta parsimonia* ('hard and strict in all things and most frugal'). Martial made a point of contrasting the civilized Greek with the austere, virile, harsh-voiced Spaniard of unkempt appearance and spontaneity. Polybius, in a like vein, compared the Iberians and North Africans, accustomed to and delighting in a harsh mode of life, to the Gaulish Celts 'of little endurance'.

Of the two-dimensional arts, unfortunately, not much survives, in comparison with monumental remains, from this formative period of Roman occupation. Much of the work of higher quality, it must be assumed, was imported from the Metropolis. One work, no doubt of native provenance, is a mosaic which graphically describes a circus scene, uncovered in Barcelona, which though crude in technique quivers with the intense, dynamic and sanguinary action of the Games. It is precisely this general Roman veristic sense which, in the arts, is probably its greatest, although latent, legacy to later Spanish imagery.

Circus. Floor mosaic, *c.* 100 BC. Archaeological Museum, Barcelona.

2   *The Rise of Christian Spain: AD 200 to 1300*

The fate of Roman rule in Hispania paralleled that of the Metropolis, as did the rise of Christianity. The Church was already institutionalized by the beginning of the third century in Spain, although occasional repressions early gave rise to a pantheon of native martyrs: Sta Eulalia of Mérida, St Vincent of Saguntum and St Severons of Barcelona. The respite and recognition given the Church by Constantine were due in part to the guidance given the Emperor by his spiritual adviser, the Bishop Hosius (or Ossius) of Córdoba, a notable opponent of that Arian heresy which opposed the Catholic dogma of the indivisible nature of *Pater et Filio Sancti*. Spain was early asserting its role in Catholicism.

It was the Iberian-born Emperor Theodosius' son Honorius who was instrumental in settling Germanic tribes (emigrating originally from Sweden by way of Gotland, hence, 'Goths') within the Empire, leading eventually to the difficult and tenuous establishment of a Visigothic Spain, from the later fifth century, with its capital in Toledo. As many of the emigrants were of the Arian persuasion this gave rise to an opposing 'catholic' party which to further their religious convictions – and, it should be added, their dynastic ambitions – invited the aid and succour of the Byzantine Emperor Justinian's troops who forthwith (AD 554) occupied Southern Spain.

In general, we can characterize the Visigothic period as a barbaric, teutonic admixture of moribund Roman art and culture and eastern display, as is evidenced by the lavish finds of crowns, swords and other valuable metalwork, such as those of Guarràzar Treasure. Unfortunately, there is little, if anything, in the way of painting which has survived the Arab deprivations. The effect of the Visigothic element on later Asturian and Mozarabic art must not be dismissed lightly, but our knowledge of the prime source of

16

the latter must remain conjectural. There is, in the Bibliothèque Nationale in Paris, a manuscript known as the *Ashburnham Pentateuch* which is often cited as possibly having been executed in seventh-century Spain and which, if so, shows Spain to have been a link with the equally conjectural art of Christian North Africa. But one can rest upon surer ground by illustrating a stone carving from the seventh-century church of Sta María de Quintanilla de las Viñas (Burgos) which relies upon the same mode of rude, linear schematization which, when coupled with vivid and flat colours, will be carried on in later Mozarabic painting.

Visigoth splendour and wealth also encouraged such endeavours as Archbishop Isadore (d. AD 636) of Seville's *Etymologies*, in twenty volumes, which compilation was to be of such great use to the nascent scholarship of the whole of Europe; to this day almost a thousand manuscript copies have survived.

In AD 711, one of the most decisive events in Spanish history took place: 12,000 Berbers, Arabs and Syrians, under Tarik,

Two Angels holding a Representation of the Sun. Visigoth, end of the seventh century. Relief on abacus slab, from the Hermitage Chapel of Santa María, Quintanilla de las Viñas (Burgos). *in situ.*

Representation of a Tower-shaped Fortress, with Three Angels or Warriors above, and with Various Figures placed in the middle part of the Tower in three Superimposed Files. Miniature painting from the *Codex Emilianensis*, AD 994. Escorial.

landed at Gibraltar (*Jebel-al-Tarik*: 'Tarik's Mount'), and, due to the internal fractionalization of the Visigoths, quickly set about occupying the Peninsula. In AD 718, under the Asturian king Pelayo, the reconquest (*Reconquista*) was initiated, thereby commencing nearly eight centuries of conflict and ideological bloodshed. A tenth-century parchment manuscript, the *Codex Emilianensis*, depicts the Christians, guarded by armed saints, after having driven the Moors from a church (note the architectural motif of the Visigothic 'horseshoe' arch later to be used, in modified form, by Arab and Gothic architects).

The *Reconquista* is the unrelenting *idée-fixe* of the Spanish Middle Ages and the crucible in which Spanish honour and aggressive, yet noble and aristocratic, chivalry were forged. It could be argued that the spirit of the *Reconquista* did not terminate with the capture of Granada, in 1492, and the subsequent expulsion of the Moors, but indeed supplied the impulsive power for the *Conquistadores* of a New World with the eventual assimilation, through tenacious daring, ideological intensity and hard-learnt military prowess, of millions of American Indians into the Church and the Hispanic way of life.

The surviving Visigothic nobility, retreating into the strongholds of the northern mountains, founded the beleaguered Kingdom of Asturias (capital, Oviedo); they entered culturally what might be called a Pre-Romanesque phase which is roughly contemporaneous with the first burst of Caliphal splendour, in Córdoba. The influences of the Carolingian *renovatio* are felt in Aragon and Catalonia where Charlemagne created a 'Spanish March', or buffer-state against Islam, following the reverses at Roncesvalles (AD 778), epically treated in the *Chanson de Roland*.

An illuminated page from the *Codex Vigilano* (AD 976) demonstrates how the rulers of the recent Kingdoms of León and Asturias attempted to symbolize the continuity of their lineage from the late Visigoth house. In the palatine chapel of San Julián de Los Prados, Santullano (Oviedo), built between AD 812 and 842, is one of the most surprising examples of the survival of Antique forms in the early Middle Ages. Although the mural paintings were

*The Visigoth Kings: Chindasvinthus, Recesvinthus and Egica; and the Asturian–
Leonese Rulers: Urraca, Sancho, and Ramiro; with the Scribes: Sarracino, Vigila,
and Garsea.* Miniature from the *Codex Vigilano* (or *Albeldense*), AD 976. Escorial.

completely decayed, careful investigations in this century have enabled a reconstruction of this example of Carolingian contact which, expressing Aragonese imperial pretensions, revives the illusionistic techniques of Roman architectural vistas, perhaps derivative of the antique theatrical backdrops for tragedy, and similar to the Ravenna mosaics. The solemn repetition of *aediculae* (recesses) appears to symbolize the thirty-eight churches, whose reunion alludes to the national Councils, nucleus of an embattled Christian Spain.

From the end of the ninth century there is evidence, in art and architecture, of that Mozarabic art which is a blending of a multiplicity of styles – Arabic, Asturian, Visigothic, Byzantine and Ibero-Roman – and which early manifests the perennial Spanish genius for assimilation and synthesis. In this truly Hispanic fusion of the European and the Oriental, we find the first works which can, in all truth, be said to mark a clearly 'national style'. Further, the Mozarabic style is to be, as many scholars contend, one of the major foundations upon which the Romanesque rests. The term itself is of disputed origin; some say it comes either from the Castilian, *mozos de los árabes* (arabic subjects), or from the Arabic, *musta 'rib* (arabized). Suffice to say, it was equally practised in the Islamic South (where tolerance was often extended to practising Christians) and in the Christian North (where such benevolence and charity was rather more wanting).

In painting it is a style which tends towards bright, unmodulated patterns and colours, and areas bounded by stiff and precise linear contours; it is planar in the extreme. Islamic influence is specifically to be seen in the design-like rendition of animals and in the conventional poses and drapery of prophets. The most influential of the Mozarabic manuscripts, copiously copied from the ninth through the thirteenth centuries, and widely diffused beyond the Pyrenees, is the celebrated *Commentary on the Apocalypse of St John*, compiled by the Abbot Beatus of Liébana in AD 716, while preoccupied with the imminent end of the world. It appears that *The Apocalypse* was a book which – for its visionary flavour: strange figures, dreams and terrifying landscapes, making it the

Woman on the Beast. Miniature from the *Apocalypse* or *Beato of Liébana,* AD 975.
Cathedral, Gerona.

Crucifixion. Miniature from the *Apocalypse* or *Beato of Liébana*, AD 975. Cathedral, Gerona.

The Symbol of St John the Evangelist above with Two Angels below. Miniature on parchment, later twelfth century. Diocesan Museum, Gerona.

most fantastic and imaginative book in all Christian literature – was already held in great favour in the Visigothic era. Thus these Mozarabic miniatures, without much doubt, hark directly back to that earlier art the spirit and form of which, in painting, we can only clearly discern in these popular remains.

Characteristically enough, its popularity appears in Spain to antedate, by some four centuries, that universal European fascination with the Apocalypse from the twelfth century on. There are, complete or in fragments, dozens of codices with illustrations to the *Beato*, or the Book of Daniel, which so widely influenced later miniature painting in addition to greatly amplifying the iconography of both the two-dimensional and the plastic arts of the later Middle Ages. Within the *Beato* format itself, one can trace the stylistic changes to the full Romanesque style, as developed in Spain from the eleventh century, by comparing a later twelfth-century *Beato*; although the textual source is the same, one is now confronted with the maturity of the sophisticated, monumental and majestic style paralleled by the Compostelan sculptural decorations.

In any discussion of Spanish illuminations, no matter how brief, one must at least mention the later charming and evocative illustrations to the varied compilations, similar in their ambitions to Isadore's *Etymologies*, of Alfonso X, 'The Learned' (1221–84), which deal with such diverse subjects as courtly rule and decorum, gaming and Spanish and universal history.

An interesting and rare example of the Mozarabic style translated into a monumental idiom is to be seen in the remains of the fresco cycle from San Baudelio, Casillas de Berlanga (Soria), which date from the beginnings of the eleventh century. While the frescoes were removed from the chapel in 1926 and sent to form part of various collections in the United States, a 'Stag Hunt' has been recently returned, by the New York Metropolitan Museum, to the Prado on an indefinite loan. Although the majority of the themes depicted in the original ensemble treated of evangelical subjects, some purely secular subjects were also depicted. The style of the work here illustrated is much less linear than the purely religious subjects and creates its forceful impression through a use of firm

Alfonso X amongst Courtiers, with a Scribe and Villagers. Miniature from the *Tratado de Juegos de Ajedrez, dados y tablas,* 1221–84. Monastery Library, Escorial.

Stag Hunt. Mural painting originally from the Mozarabic Church of San Baudelio de Casillas de Berlanga (Soria), first part of the eleventh century. Museo del Prado, Madrid.

outline and superimposed, unmodelled, almost heraldic imagery and regularized spacing.

The eventual emergence of the full Romanesque style in Spain can be explained by reference to political and religious events occurring outside the artistic field. The repression of the Mozarabic Christians within 'Al-Andalus' itself and the aggressive policies of the Caliph Hixem's prime minister, Almanzor, without provoked renewed counter-attacks – following Muslim attacks on Barcelona (AD 985) and Santiago de Compostela (AD 997) – from the beleaguered kingdoms of the north. After a great deal of difficulty, the Christians finally were able to form a military alliance capable of overturning the Caliphate (1032), and those areas remaining under Islamic sway broke up into the *taifas* while León joined with Asturias to create the brief 'Empire' of Sancho the Great of Navarre. In the mid-eleventh century, therefore, a seemingly united Christian Spain was able to initiate diplomatic and ecclesiastical relations with Europe and, as a result, the various Italian and French religious orders were to establish reforming centres south of the Pyrenees bringing in their wake a taste for the monumental, the evangelical and the magnificent.

The full splendour of Spanish Romanesque painting, unique in Europe for its quantity and preservation, is to be seen in the fresco cycles. Some of the finest of these works are now preserved in the Museum of Catalan Art in Barcelona. Their survival has been due to their location in the poetic heights of the Pyrenees where they were protected from the vicissitudes of war and fashion in such humble and provincial churches as that of San Clemente de Tahull. The interior magnificences of its apse mural is surprising. This large, brightly-hued painting reflects with almost primitive vigour its selective character evidencing what is in effect provincial stringent economy, the by then thoroughly internationalized Byzantine manner. The creation of this anonymous 'Master of Tahull' is central to the emerging Spanish tradition in its clear attempt to reduce the sophisticated complexities of the imported compositional pattern to one at once more simple and yet more thoroughly stylized. There is a dominant effect of close-knit unity, and a clear and

The Pantokrator with the Symbols of the Four Evangelists, Angels, and Saints: Luke, Bartholomew, Mary, John and James. Romanesque mural paintings originally from the central apse of the Church of San Clemente de Tahull (Lérida), early twelfth century. Museum of Catalan Art, Barcelona.

The Creation of Adam and the Original Sin. Romanesque wall painting, originally from the hermitage chapel of La Cruz de Maderuelo (Segovia), *c.* 1125. Museo del Prado, Madrid.

ponderous rhythm enhances the stern, austere expressionism of the central image of the Pantokrator; the total effect is one of boldness and majesty.

Another interesting direction in Romanesque mural painting is manifested in the extremely schematic and linear treatment of the nude to be seen in a section of the frescoes (*c.* 1125) from the main chapel of the Church of the Holy Cross, Maderuelo (Segovia). These Castilian works, supposedly by a colleague of the Tahull Master, demonstrate a possible Mozarabic dilution in the diffusion of his forceful style. Like the Pyrenean cycles they have been removed from their original location, transferred to a canvas backing, and are now – in this case – handsomely presented in the Prado. This appearance of the nude is unique for the period. The emphatic tracery of the figures of Adam and Eve reveals clearly the abstracting, un-empirical and design-oriented modes of the medieval craftsman-artisan. It also evidences the subordination of anatomy and plastic appearance to overriding principles of compositional vitality and rhythmic integration, principles still operable in, for instance, the work of Picasso in our own time.

An early instance of the persistent Spanish taste for realism and the expressionistic, based upon an almost clinical and cold-blooded observation and dissection of form and content, is to be seen in an altar frontal, or antependium, depicting the martyrdom of Sta Julita and her son St Quiricus (mid-twelfth century). This form of emergent narrative art, like – in a different manner – the charming illustrations to the works of Alfonso 'El Sabio', which represent an early anti-Byzantine and anti-monumental direction in Spanish painting, is perhaps derived from English miniatures of the Bury St Edmunds scriptorium or, perhaps, the sculpture of Vézelay and Autun.

The Life and Martyrdom of Santa Julita and her son St Quiricus. Painted wooden antependium, from the hermitage church of Santa Julita de Durro, Valle de Boí (Lérida), twelfth century. Museum of Catalan Art, Barcelona.

Funeral Procession. Painted wooden panel from the sepulchre of the knight Sainz Carillo, from Mahamud (Burgos), early fourteenth century. Museum of Catalan Art, Barcelona.

The Spanish Romanesque period is especially rich and dramatic; its severity of form and grave nobility of content was expressive of Iberian sobriety and ethical purpose. One of the clearest, most dramatic examples of this spirit is to be seen in a painted panel from the tomb of Don Sancho Saíz de Castillo, from Mahamud (Burgos) from the beginnings of the fourteenth century. One can almost hear the keening of the anguished mourners, and the jagged linear distortions and expressionistic liberties seem to strangely foreshadow the *Guernica* of over five centuries later.

Pablo **Picasso** *Guernica.* Lithograph, 1937. Museum of Modern Art. New York.

3 Late Medieval and Early Renaissance Spain: 1300 to 1500

In the second quarter of the fourteenth century, there was initiated in Barcelona and Valencia, facing Italy and always receptive to her innovations, that style which – for more or less faithfully echoing the *Trecento* – is known as Italo-Gothic. In a fresco cycle by Ferrer Bassa, in the Monastery of Pedralbes (Barcelona), 1345–56, one notes the imitation of Giotto's manner – recalling, specifically in format and technique, the Arena Chapel – thereby introducing into Spanish painting a sense of sculptural bulk and strength. However, the Spanish Giottesques (and later painters) lacked, on the one hand, the Italian sense of the ideal – that tendency towards

Ferrer Bassa *The Nativity*. Wall painting, in oils, from the Chapel of San Miguel in the cloister of the Monastery of Pedralbes (Barcelona), 1346. *in situ.*

Pedro Serra *Altarpiece of the Holy Spirit*. The Church of Santa Maria, Manresa (Barcelona), *c.* 1394. *in situ.*

the typological and the archaeological – and, on the other, Italian classicist strivings after perfection of form and finish. As Oskar Hagen has pointed out, 'the model and its imitation compare as the guttural Spanish compares with the sonorous Italian'.

As, however, was the case in Siena and Tuscany, the plastic Giottesque style was soon to be supplanted by the anecdotal charms, mannered elegance and compositional irrelevancies of the International Style. This femininely sinuous and petitely rhythmic style, with its heightened interest in genre detail, is well exemplified by Pedro Serra's *Altarpiece of the Holy Spirit* (1394). Serra belongs to the Valencian school, traditionally the most suave and gentle, like its levantine climate, of the Spanish regional schools.

Although – militarily, politically and economically – Islamic Spain was in the throes of its final decline (until 1492), it was to exercise in art a lasting influence long after its temporal demise. Elements of moorish style, as they influenced and were assimilated by Christian artists, belong to *Mudéjar* art – from the Arabic *mudayan*, or 'subjugated'. Although Mohammedans were obliged to either emigrate or become Catholics (by law, in 1502, in Castille and León; and 1526 in Aragón) their traditions lived on in Spanish art. The converts were known as *moriscos*, which, in turn, is sometimes used as a stylistic term.

As late as 1633, an influential treatise (on carpentry) by Diego López de Arenas advocated the continuance of Islamic techniques and modes. It is precisely this moorish residue which, in part, explains the persistently anti-classical nature of Spanish art. This 'arabization' of Spanish art is evident in the reliquary triptych of 1390, from the Monastery of Piedra. The painting itself, Serresque, is well within the International Gothic style; however, the enframing ensemble, determining its overall spirit, is one of the finest extant examples of moorish carving and shows direct affinities with the fourteenth-century architectural décor of the magical Alhambra (Granada).

Reinforced by Islamic practices, certainly congenial to the Spanish mood and vision if not their ultimate creator, Spanish art has persisted, to our times, in formal solutions based upon accentuated

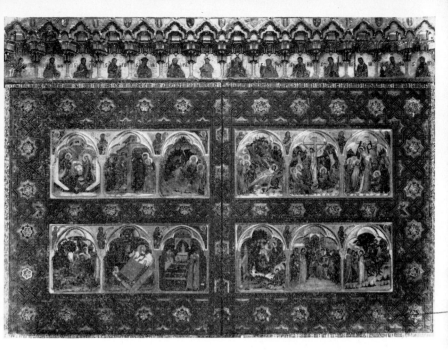

Reliquary chest, from the Monastery of Piedra (Zaragoza), with the doors closed showing the painted panels, 1390. Royal Academy of History, Madrid.

rhythmic patternings, geometric stylizations, planar suppression of space, ornate and decorative monumentality, and – in content – a melancholic resignation and hieratic, aristocratic magnificence. The celebrated historian of Spanish painting, Chandler R. Post, has wondered if 'perhaps the Spanish artist, in spreading a soberly rich harmony of colour over his surfaces, is sometimes thinking in terms of an oriental rug'.

Two works from the second half of the fifteenth century, by Bartolomé Bermejo and Jaime Huguet, when Spanish painting was under the sway of the precisions of Flemish realism, also reveal, despite the naturalistic portrayal of the individual, the taste for a compositional rigidity which breaks up the picture into almost

37

Bartolomé Bermejo *Santo Domingo de Silos*. Panel painting, *c.* 1477. Museo del Prado, Madrid.

Jaime Huguet *The Episcopal Consecration of St Augustine.* Panel painting which originally formed part of the 'Retablo of the Tanners' Guild of Barcelona', *c.* 1480. Museum of Catalan Art, Barcelona.

symmetrical patterns, a trait perhaps provoked by the pure design of moorish decoration. However, in the dichotomy between the face and its surroundings, there is evidence of another perennial Hispanic trait: pronounced realism, especially in the objective analysis of individual character. This is a popular feature, too, in Spanish literature from the Middle Ages on, manifested as early as the anonymous *Poema del Cid*, of *c.* 1140, which contrasts so strongly with its fantastical contemporary, the *Chanson de Roland*.

In these works, one might assume by extension that the relative flatness of the ensemble is specifically employed to throw the face into heightened relief and, hence, the persistence of gold (and, later, neutral) backgrounds in Spanish portraiture through the Baroque period. Faithfulness to the model was always more evident than in Italian art which tended to idealize, or search for a universal type. But the Spaniard delighted in the unique, the eccentric and the characteristic. However, it is the union of realism of *essential* (characteristic) detail and an often highly stylized design and setting, which is one of the hallmarks of Spanish vision.

One would not, however, wish to give the impression that an anachronistic use of gilded backgrounds is the only characteristic of fifteenth-century Spanish painting. In the work of the Salamancan-born Fernando Gallego (1440/45–after 1507), the first influential master of the nascent Castilian School, landscape is accepted as an integral and eloquent part of composition. Gallego was strongly influenced by the drama of Flemish and German naturalism, particularly the work of Dirk Bouts and Martin Schongauer (which does not, however, imply that he ever left Spain or even, for that matter, Castille). His highly personal style was innovative and widely disseminated, even as far south as Extremadura. For Gallego, these Northern influences were only a point of departure in the forming of his own brand of heightened, almost primitive, realism which expressed itself melodramatically in twisted poses, extreme facial expressions and contortions, and in an overall, most uncomfortable angularity as clearly shown in his *Pietà* (before 1467). These expressionistic devices and his concern with simplified repeated textures and surfaces – tying the whole surface of the painted panel together by means of wiry, sinuous rhythms – indicate a resurgence of the Spanish search for eloquent forms which transcend their superficial decorative significance.

In Bermejo's later *Pietà*, personally signed ('Opus Bartolomeus Vermejo Cordubensis') and dated 1490, following by a decade and a half his *St Dominic of Silos*, one sees a further extension of the expressionistic sensibility and of spatial usages rather like that of those Flemish masters who followed the Van Eycks, Roger van der Weyden, and Bouts such as Hugo dan der Goes and Geertgen tot Sint Jans. This *Pietà* is especially unique, however, in foreshadowing

Fernando Gallego *Pietà* (or *The Fifth Anguish*), signed 'Fernandus Gallecus'. Panel painting, *c.* 1465. Museo del Prado, Madrid.

sixteenth-century movements. It is the practice of art historians to signal Giorgione's famous *Tempestà* (*c.* 1505), early works of Altdorfer such as his *Satyr Family* (*c.* 1507) or his *St George in a Wood* (*c.* 1510), or even Patinir's *Charon Crossing the Styx* (*c.* 1520–25) as being the earliest examples of the dominance of landscape over figures as the major conveyor of 'mood' in painting. But the Bermejo work clearly antedates such developments and, further, it must be assumed that it was conceived without any direct knowledge of any earlier Venetian or Northern works exhibiting such tendencies.

Bartolomé Bermejo *The Pietà of Canon Desplá*. Panel painting, *c.* 1490. Cathedral, Barcelona.

This work depicts the stubble-bearded donor, Canon Lluis Desplá kneeling on the right, with veristic harshness and a great amount of psychological acumen. Here, for the first time in Spanish painting, the donor's facial expression and attitude indicate his full participation in the Christian drama. Both Desplá and St Jerome, on the Virgin's right hand, serve compositionally as anguished brackets to the central pairing of Mary lamenting over the stiffly rigid, bloodied body of her martyred Son. While the figure types are rather Netherlandish, the sombre, brownish coloration and emphasized silhouetting of the dark figures is emphatically Spanish. But, above all, the principal dramatic vehicle is the darkening, troubled sky with its flickering lights and startled flights of birds; it prefigures the emotional turmoil and unease which was to universally afflict European art some decades later. In the particularly local sense, however, Bermejo's *Pietà* seems to reflect aspects of that pronounced transcendental emotionalism – or 'mysticism' – which becomes evident in Spanish literature of the end of the fifteenth century.

These dramatic works provide an illuminating insight into the peculiarities of the Hispano-Flemish style. Its wholesale acceptance in Spain after 1460–70 is due in large part to external events. The Aragonese rulers had been successful in extending their sphere of influence into Italy after having established a Sicilian beachhead from the end of the thirteenth century; their traditional policy was that of a *Drang nach Osten* or 'drive to the east'. This was modified by a shift in policy to the 'drive to the north' when the Houses of Aragón and Castille were joined in marriage in 1469; and Ferdinand and Isabella were eventually to join their tragic daughter, 'Juana la Loca', to Phillip the Fair, heir to the northern Hapsburg dominions. A massive importation of Netherlandish work and artists in central and northern Spain indicates a shift in taste paralleling the shift of power towards these areas. The realism of the Flemish style was obviously a more practical vehicle to express the Spanish taste for the particular and the concrete than the mannered whimsy of the Italo-Gothic.

Universally cited as the first evidence of the Hispano-Flemish

Luis Dalmáu *The Madonna of Councílors*. Tempera and oil on panel, 1443–5. Museum of Catalan Art, Barcelona.

hybrid is a work of 1445 by Luis Dalmáu: *The Madonna of Councílors*, commissioned for the Barcelona Town Hall. This work seems a direct reflection of Jan van Eyck's visits of 1427 and 1428; and it is obviously modelled upon that master's *Ghent Altarpiece* and his *Madonna of Canon van der Paele*, the latter work of only a decade before. However, Dalmáu flattens the flowing plasticity of his models, rejecting volume in favour of stiff linearisms; also the Spaniard is much more straightforward and less subtle. The absence of 'disguised symbolism', such a marked trait of Flemish sophistication, is typical of the Spanish preference for a more immediate and direct statement, just as the Spanish artist and patron preferred to conceive of their religious experience in a less than roundabout fashion. Rather than subtle moral allegories and recondite symbolic rebuses, an emphatic narrative and sensory rendering of a given saint's 'life' and tragedies was demanded.

There are also most revealing *formal* divergences from the Flemish 'norm': the varied brilliance of Northern colour is consistently replaced by muted tonalities; breadth of spatial illusionism, as mentioned, is generally renounced in favour of two-dimensionality and crowded surfaces; the precision of the miniaturist's technique is exchanged for a cruder, more spontaneous and broader kind of brushwork; attention is often focused upon the face at the expense of the rest of the ensemble creating a hypnotic frontality; balance of gesture and poses gives way to emphatic movements and expressions.

One might have occasion here to treat of that celebrated Hispanic taste for the 'gruesome', now made especially graphic through Renaissance realism. There are, in Spanish painting, any number of sanguinary martyrdoms (both religious and, later, political). They arise, in part, from excesses of the gravity of the Spanish character which does tend towards the pessimistic – in a lighter vein, in literature, this can be seen in the sardonically humorous extravagances of Don Quixote, in the *socarronería* (irony) of Galdós, in the nineteenth-century novel or in similar effects of the contemporary author Cela, etc. Its darker side is often a morbid, but sober, gloom. It is life observed and pain is, in this case, exemplary and transcendental. It is this spirit, I feel, which lies behind the terminal drama of the bullfight. As in a great deal of Spanish art, one must look behind the superficial carnage and revulsion to find the persistent strain of a moral rigour and an essentially stoic and impassive, objectivized narration which elevates the subject beyond what may seem mere sensationalism. The imagery is, without doubt, often horrible but it is also, to the Spaniard, edifying.

The greatest splendour, and most relevatory of Spanish systems within the Renaissance, is to be seen in the *retablos* (sometimes

Ayne Bru (Heinrich Brün?) *The Martyrdom of St Cucufat*. Panel painting which formed part of the great Altarpiece of Sant Cugat del Vallés, 1502–6. Museum of Catalan Art, Barcelona.

46

Francisco Goya *The Third of May: The Executions on the Príncipe Pío Hill.* Oil on canvas, *c.* 1814. Museo del Prado, Madrid.

'retables' or 'reredos'), contemporaneous with the advent of the High Renaissance, and after, in Italy. These are the tremendous agglomerations of polychrome, panel painting, gilt, stucco and wood which form so dramatic a backdrop to the celebrations of the mystic rites of the Mass.

Stylistically, they fall within the traditional affection for the 'carpet-like' and demonstrate characteristics of *horror vacui* (the dislike of empty or free space) and are edged and tied together by wiry geometric arabesques with angular, stressed borders which develop a cellular repetition of themes and motifs creating the unremittent movement typical, too, of the traditional variational

Gil de Silos. The main altarpiece in the Carthusian Monastery of Miraflores (Burgos), *c.* 1496–9. *in situ.*

Façade of the Church of San Esteban Salamanca. Designed by Juan de Alava and finished by Juan de Rivero, Pedro Gutierrez y Diego de Salcedo, *c.* 1524–1610.

form of Spanish music, both popular and classical. The inflexible and harsh framework can be said to express the reticence and conservatism of the Spaniard, while the glistening mass, which swallows up the details, harks to the native love of grave pomp and ritualistic display. Stylistically, the *retablos* belong to the 'Plateresque' (in the manner of a silversmith) conventions of architectural design, to such an extent that the external façade becomes constructed upon the same principles, creating a stylistic homogeneity between inside and outside.

4 *Mannerism and Anti-Mannerism in Spanish Painting of the Sixteenth Century*

It must be kept in mind that Spain, in the modern political sense, has only been in existence from the very end of the fifteenth century after the uniting of Castille and Aragón through the marriage of Ferdinand and Isabel, the 'Catholic Monarchs' (*los Reyes Católicos*). In 1478 the Inquisition was renewed in Spain and, fourteen years later, the *Reconquista* was completed and Columbus had been sent to discover a new world. In 1519, two years after his arrival in Spain, Carlos I was elected emperor of the Holy Roman Empire under the name of Charles V. Under the Hapsburgs, while Spain (and the Empire) extended their power and prestige throughout Europe, Africa and the Americas, there commenced that unending series of entanglements and warfare – both dynastic and religious – which dissipated Spanish wealth, manpower and morale. It is against this uneasy and unstable background that the impressive achievements of the Spanish Renaissance and *Siglo de Oro* took place.

One might wonder precisely what 'Renaissance' means in its Spanish application. Interestingly enough, the phrase 'the period of the Renaissance' occurs in Ford's *Handbook of Spain* (1845) some ten years before Michelet's *La Renaissance* and fifteen before Jacob Burckhardt's well known Italian application of the same in *Die Kultur der Renaissance in Italien* (1860). While the notion of a 'revival under the influence of classical models' was conceived and formulated by Petrarch (1304–74), with the novelties of periodization (*historiae antiquae* and *historiae novae*: 'ancient' vs 'modern' times), one hesitates to apply the period term, in the Italian sense, to Spanish art. As shall be seen there are abundant formal reasons for wondering if such a phenomenon as the 'High Renaissance Style' really occurred in Spain to parallel the Italian movement. Also, it is well to recall the strong gravitational pull of tradition,

Pedro Berruguete *Auto Da Fé presided over by Sto Domingo de Guzmán*. Panel, *c.* 1490. Museo del Prado, Madrid.

in this case rooted in the Middle Ages, which is such a constant force of Spanish culture.

In Italy the 'return to nature' had exercised a major role in painting, whereas the 'return to classical antiquity', from Brunelleschi on, was paramount in architecture, due logically enough to the plenitude of actual examples. Of course, in the case of painting there was no first-hand knowledge of actual antique practices, as the Roman frescoes of Pompeii and Herculaneum were not to be brought to light until the eighteenth century. It is thus noteworthy that, if architecture was early the most 'classical' of the reborn arts, in Spain sixteenth-century treatises on architecture continued to refer to what we now know as the Gothic style as 'modern' (cf. particularly Cristóbal de Villalón, *Ingeniosa Comparación entre lo antiguo y lo presente*, Valladolid, 1539; Juan de Arfe, *Varia Comensuración, para la escultura y arquitectura*, Seville, 1585; and Alonso de Vandelvira's roughly contemporaneous *Libro de Trazas de Piedras*) long after that term, in Italy, had been employed for the full classicism of the High Renaissance. Further, the Spanish use of 'classical' motifs mostly dealt with *grotesques* (from the painted decorations discovered in the 'grottoes' of Nero's *Domus Aurea*) which express a most 'unclassical' and decorative manner.

Further, if, as Vasari stated, the requirements of Italian classicism were rule, order, measure, design and 'manner' (a given artist's 'type' of beauty), a good case could be made for the suggestion that these went against the grain of the essentially spontaneous, naturalistically oriented and 'unaesthetic' practices and creeds of the Spanish painter. In short, and in Italian terms, Spaniards lacked *gentilezza, doctrina, mesure* and *vera proportione*.

Certainly the sudden explosion of Imperial militaristic power was such that Spanish culture (as, for instance, can be seen in its painting) had for about a century much difficulty in keeping pace with it or, for that matter, in creating for itself a viable synthesis between old and new. Artistic endeavour, due in part to the lack of organized, established and munificent patronage, was extremely scattered and hardly comparable to the Italian pattern. Then too

53

the direction of Italian art, with its emphasis on idealism and anti-quarianism, tended to ignore the simple and unpretentious directions favoured by Spanish realistic immediacy. Also, as has been pointed out, both the conservative nature and traditionally anti-classical character of Spanish art militated against an *understanding* of the essence of the Roman High Renaissance, no matter how much lip-service was paid to its obvious prestige and attractiveness. Certainly, searching for an adequate expression to the demands of an obviously 'new age', the Spanish artists who *attempted* Italianate exercises were many; but, by temperament and tradition, they yet remained Spanish.

Although Spain as a whole welcomed the Italian Renaissance and Humanism during the first quarter of the *Cinquecento* with a fervour perhaps unmatched elsewhere, the fundamental character of Spanish painting persisted in *mudéjar* and gothic anachronisms. One finds that, for the most part, the High Renaissance yielded to the more emotional style of Mannerism – and I am referring particularly to its earlier phase, which might conveniently be called a 'Counter-Renaissance' movement (in effect, gothicizing reversion) which is seen in Italian art from about 1515–45 – precisely because, in its medievalisms and expressionism, it proved itself to be much more congenial to the Spanish character than the calm perfection, balanced harmonies and, above all, Olympian distance of Italian full classicism.

Let us then look to what might be construed as 'pure classical' Spanish works precisely in order to cite their divergences from the 'norm'. Pedro Berruguete (*c.* 1450–1504), a major figure in the Castilian School and father of Alonso Berruguete who will be discussed later, was chronologically the first of the 'italianizing' painters. In a work (*c.* 1480) which he did at the court of Federico da Montefeltro, Duke of Urbino, one can appreciate his thorough comprehension of the Italian – and classical – integration of plastic figures in space. And yet one notes that after his return to Spain (*c.* 1483), he reverted, to some extent, to those traditional portrait conventions already discussed. Another Castilian master, Juan de Borgoña (*c.* 1470–1536), probably of Burgundian origins, shows

Pedro Berruguete *Federico da Montefeltro, Duke of Urbino, and his son Guido-baldo*. Panel, *c.* 1480. National Gallery, Urbino.

REX SALAMON

Pedro Berruguete *King Solomon*. Panel painting, part of the main altarpiece of the Church of Santa Eulalia, Paredes de Nava (Palencia), *c.* 1485. *in situ.*

Juan de Borgoña *The Embrace of Saints Jochim and Anne before the Golden Gate.* Mural painting in the Capitular Hall of the Cathedral, Toledo. *c.* 1509–11.

the attempt to assimilate figures into architectural settings, but the proportions of the latter are often disconcerting and the central personages tend to assume rigid, ritualistic poses.

Valencia, as might be expected, was early to receive Italian influences. The anonymous (possibly by Rodrigo de Osona, the Elder)

Rodrigo de Osona (?) (or Paolo Sancto Leocadio ?) *Madonna of the Knight of Montesa, with Saints Benito and Bernard*. Panel, *c.* 1485. Museo del Prado, Madrid.

Madonna of the Knight of Montesa c. 1485, in its balance and architectural background harks back to late *Quattrocento* modes but the wooden gestures, stiff draperies, startling colour and studied facial types betray its peninsular origins. In the work of another Valencian, Fernando Yáñez (fl. 1506–36), there are clearly stated Leonardesque

Fernando Yáñez de la Almedina *St John the Baptist*. Panel, *c.* 1510. Prats Tomás
Collection, Barcelona.

Fernando Yáñez de la Almedina *St Catherine*. Panel, *c.* 1515. Museo del Prado, Madrid.

directions but also a peculiar spatial sense and a nervous self-consciousness and intensity unknown to the Italian. In his famous *St Catherine*, in the Prado, he has created a masterpiece but the stage-set like handling of the architecture and the curvilinear arabesques of the drapery designs are indigenous qualities.

In the second third of the century, one becomes aware of the beginnings of *maniera* in the Italian sense of the word: the deliberate adoption of another's style. Again, Valencian masters took the lead. In Vicente Masip's *Martyrdom of St Agnes* (*c.* 1535), the rhetoric, figure crowding and compression, deliberately confusing

Vicente Masip *The Martyrdom of St Agnes*. Panel, *c.* 1535. Museo del Prado, Madrid.

composition, unclear space and contorted postures – which arose in large part out of the later School of Raphael – become apparent. One sees here the artificial attempt to stylize style itself. In the work of Masip's son Juan de Juanes (*c.* 1523–79) there is a somewhat calmer use of Italian models, particularly in his interesting rendition of *The Last Supper* (*c.* 1570), taken from Marcantonio's print of Leonardo's fresco. However, the spatial sense is altered by the intrusion of objects in the foreground which purposely detract from the essential action and, further, serve to 'planarize' the whole. Interestingly, Juanes departs from the model also in rejecting Leonardo's theatrical treatment of the drama of Christ's denunciation to concentrate instead upon the mystic revelation in the gesture of the Saviour's symbolic presentation of his flesh in the Eucharist. However, perhaps more successfully than most, Juanes was able to adopt and intensify the external features of Italian classicism, in particular, the larger compositional format; nevertheless, in his greater religious – as opposed to aesthetic and formalistic – concerns, he departed characteristically from his foreign sources.

We shall now backtrack a little to discuss two Spaniards who,

Juan de Juanes *The Last Supper*. Panel, *c.* 1570. Museo del Prado, Madrid.

Pedro Machuca *The Deposition*. Panel (from the appearance of the original frame, it probably served as a small altarpiece in an unknown locale), before 1520 (?). Museo del Prado, Madrid.

according to Roberto Longhi and others, were instrumental in the creation of Mannerism within the High Renaissance style, *in Italy itself*; in fact, they are cited as being the first non-Italians to employ, consistently, that style. Pedro Machuca (end of the fifteenth century – 1550) exhibits in his panel of *The Desposition*, which perhaps dates from his Italian apprenticeship before 1520, complications of composition and gesture and a heightened chiaroscuro, almost verging on tenebrism *à la* Caravaggio, which are reminiscent of Rosso Fiorentino. He later became an architect and is responsible for the unique – and unfinished – palace of Charles V, adjacent to the Alhambra in Granada.

Of much greater significance is Alonso Berruguete (*c.* 1488–1561) who, primarily in his capacity as a sculptor, is recognized as the greatest artist – other than El Greco – in sixteenth-century Spain. He was in Italy from *c.* 1504 to 1518 and was well known to Michelangelo, being mentioned on occasion in his correspondence; he is also cited five times by Vasari (as 'Alonso Spagnuolo'). A work from his Italian period, the Uffizi *Salome* (*c.* 1515) reveals a religious, and possibly neurotic, intensity unmatched by his contemporaries. Here one finds an absolutely innovative system of deformation. The convulsive rhythms pull the figures expressionistically away from all references to the classical norm whereas the distortions of the Italian Mannerists were precisely calculated destructions of empirical visual appearances. In this case, if one could speak of a more or less consistently 'logical' use of Mannerist devices in Italy, then Berruguete (although possibly paralleled by the Italian Pontormo) uniquely manifests the consistently illogical 'emotional' treatment thereof, in Spain.

Berruguete, in coming from an 'extra-classical' ambience, is in fact harking back to the Gothic norm of vertical, elongated and malleable proportions, spatial renunciations, intentionally 'strange' colour systems, smoothly pneumatic surfaces and contorted spiritual expressionism. In later works, executed in Spain, these anachronistic tendencies underlie the Italian 'manner'. Although he will, rightly, be primarily remembered for his sculpture, it is as a painter that he was consistently noted in contemporary documents. One could, in all justice, call his sculpture 'painterly'; the polychromed, wooden figures writhe with flame-like movements, endeavouring to transcend the earth-bound limitations of plastic

Alonso Berruguete *Salome*. Panel, *c.* 1515. Galleria Uffizi, Florence.

form. Somehow in his sculpture, perhaps by continuing to think as a painter, he was able to be even more 'pictorial' than in his two-dimensional works which tend, it must be admitted, to be somewhat bounded by the limiting concepts of the period concerning what one can and cannot 'do' on a flat surface. It can be seen that in

Alonso Berruguete *The Birth of Christ*. Panel, formed part of the 'San Benito Altarpiece', *c.* 1530. Museum of Sculpture, Valladolid.

Alonso Berruguete *The Sacrifice of Isaac*. Polychromed wooden sculpture which formed part of the 'San Benito Altarpiece', *c.* 1530. Museum of Sculpture, Valladolid.

sculpture he was better able, in a revolutionary fashion, to renounce completely the Italian humanistic fondness for beauty of
person, correct proportions and anatomy, and spatial logic by
reverting to the intense example of Spanish Late Gothic sculpture.
As such, he is the most relevatory expression of the environment
to which El Greco, in many respects, adapted himself so well.

Spanish portraiture of the period reveals another, more rigid and
hieratic, version of Mannerism which to some degree parallels the
work of the Italian Bronzino in form, while in mood it reflects
the constraining dictates on leisure-class etiquette prescribed in
Castiglione's *Courtier* which early found favour in Spain where a
notoriously chill decorum was *de rigueur* in the Court of the Phillips.
Although initially much influenced by the Holbein-like Dutch
emigrant Antonius Mor, these court portraits are very Spanish in
their decorative and planar treatment of all but the face of the
subject, and in the reliance upon restrained, almost drab, coloration
and rigid, ritualized poses.

In the relatively well known work of Luis de Morales (*c*. 1520–86),
of Extramaduran origin, one finds another instance of an 'unaesthetic' religious emotionalism. It is worth noting that Phillip II
dismissed Morales as being 'old-fashioned'; his *retardaire* style is
essentially Late Gothic. The pathetic and boneless, although often
elegant, figures express an asceticism and mystic yearning rarely
seen in Italy. That these may not be to everyone's taste, in all
justice to Phillip, is evidenced by Carl Justi's (1920) remark that
Morales' work often seems like *scheussliche Karikaturen* ('revolting
caricatures').

And now we come to by far the best known of the painters of
Renaissance Spain, El Greco (*c*. 1541–1614). However, it must not
be forgotten that he was not of Spanish birth and only arrived in
Spain when he was over thirty-five – and already a mature artist
in his own right. Born Dominicos Theotocopulos in Candia, Crete,
where he resided, as we now know from recent research, until as
late as 1566, he was always to carry with him the non-classical and
exotic lineaments of the still-living Byzantine traditions in which
he was initially trained. He was in Venice, of which Crete was then

Antonius Mor (Antonio Moro) *Queen Mary of England, the Second Wife of Phillip II.*
Panel, *c.* 1554. Museo del Prado, Madrid.

Alonzo Sánchez Coello (attr.) *Juan de Austria*. Oil on canvas, *c.* 1580. Escorial.

Luis de Morales *Virgen de la Piedad*. Oil on canvas, *c.* 1570/80. Academy of San Fernando, Madrid.

a colony, from some time before 1570 (probably 1567); he spent two years in Rome and then returned to Venice where he stayed until 1576 whereupon, seeking a court appointment, he sailed to Spain. During his Venetian period he studied with Titian and came under the influence of Tintoretto, adapting from the former the 'grand' painterly manner and, from the latter, the mannerist play of flickering light – a rhythmically decorative motif which was congenial to his Byzantine background of patterning. During his Roman stay he became acquainted with the work of Michelangelo from whom he learned the possibilities of expressive power and movement of heroic figures, burdened with fate, in twisted poses and gestures.

In Spain he is mentioned first in the capital, Madrid, in the summer of 1577; a couple of months later he took up what was to be a permanent residence in Toledo. Toledo had been, until 1561, the political centre of Spain but when he knew it it had become, in a manner of speaking, an economic backwater although it remained the intellectual capital of the nation. Aristocratic and austerely ecclesiastical, although provincial, it proved in its slumbering intensity to be congenial to the spirit of the thoughtful Greek emigrant. Having failed to win royal favour with his *Martyrdom of St Maurice and the Theban Legion* – Phillip II preferring the native qualities of unadorned gravity and decorative reticence as evidenced by the court portraits and the chill formalism of his monastery-palace, the Escorial – El Greco settled down in disappointment in Toledo, where perhaps a lack of artistic competition and convention enabled him to pursue his own imaginative directions without the censure of local precedent. We do know that there he was reasonably successful and lived in aristocratic comfort.

His first work in Toledo, *The Holy Trinity* (*c.* 1577–9), destined for the *retablo* of the church of Santo Domingo el Antiguo and now

El Greco *Martyrdom of St Maurice and the Theban Legion*. Oil on canvas, *c.* 1580/82. Escorial.

El Greco *Toledo*. Oil on canvas, *c.* 1604/14. Metropolitan Museum of Art, New York.

El Greco *The Holy Trinity*. Oil on canvas, *c.* 1577–9. Museo del Prado, Madrid.

in the Prado, shows clear links to the modelled plasticity of Italy. In the later *Agony in the Garden* (*c.* 1585), we can appreciate the Byzantine reversion which overcame him in Toledo which, in so many respects, approximates Spanish traditions. There is a preference for harsh angularities over curves. The composition is broken up into unconnected colour fields, each of which has its own decorative significance and which are, further, often in discordant relationship with adjacent areas. Landscape is reduced to a symbolic minimum and the ground planes have been employed in a manner which defies spatial and narrative logic and, in addition, there is a marked absence of either foreshortening or superimposition. The desire for an overall pattern effect becomes obvious. The sharply delineated areas and short brushstrokes, like tesserae, and the abstracted, 'mnemonic', quality of the background again recall the Byzantine mosaics.

Also true to Byzantine (and Spanish) tradition is the use of painting as a vehicle for ideas rather than for its own sake. Thus, El Greco eschewed careful finish, as can be seen in his feverish and undisguised brushwork in which the priming is often allowed to be seen in marginal areas. This technique of El Greco, which marks the advent of the spontaneous *alla prima* method in Spain, was later to be employed, to different ends, by Velásquez and, to a more marked degree, by Goya.

Two works from his last years show how El Greco's unrestrained and unconventional search for the most personalized spiritual statement led him to even more revolutionary, anti-classical and anti-naturalistic creations. In these last visionary departures he also asserts his essential independence from Spanish tradition. In his only known choice of a 'classical' subject, or essay into mythology, the *Laocoön* (*c.* 1610), he treats that well known piece of Hellenistic statuary (which work was, incidentally, a great influence upon Alonso Berruguete, in addition to the Italian Mannerists) in a manner which almost caricaturizes the anatomical

El Greco *The Agony in the Garden*. Oil on canvas, *c.* 1585. Museum of Fine Arts, Toledo, Ohio, USA.

El Greco *Laocoön*. Oil on canvas, *c.* 1610. National Gallery, Washington, DC.

complexities and agonized writhings of the original model. In El
Greco's version, the stricken group has fallen apart, dying; the
dramatic scene is set in front of Toledo, bathed by a flickering,
other-worldly light. Another work, *The Adoration of the Shepherds*
(*c.* 1612), is also characteristic of El Greco's extremist period with
its hallucinatory approach; the noted Spanish philosopher and
critic, José Ortega y Gasset, noted that these last works look
alarmingly like 'a little matter ready to ignite'.

Until around the middle of the seventeenth century El Greco
enjoyed a certain amount of prestige in artistic circles. However
with the rise of naturalism and the marked aversion for Mannerism
in the Baroque period he fell into relative oblivion. Although he was
known, to some degree, in the Romantic period, his work was only
to be re-evaluated with the anti-naturalistic bias of the Post-

Impressionist periods. Descriptive of the mood of twentieth-century expressionism is the revival of interest in Mannerism in general and El Greco in particular. In fact, he was the first artist to be considered of major importance associated with that style (for instance, Max Dvorak's well known article of 1921: 'Ueber Greco und der Manierismus') which was then interpreted in psychological and 'spiritual' terms. Recent discussions of Mannerism have, on the other hand, preferred formalistic interpretations and placed less emphasis upon the 'neurotic'.

One can begin to appreciate, in the overview, El Greco's distance from the essential qualities of Spanish art – and particularly those of the later sixteenth century. It is worth bearing in mind that this great exponent of 'Mannerism' did his most typical works *after* the Baroque style was well under way – thus, in several ways, he himself is an anachronism. One can date the first stirrings of reaction against the style to which he paid his tardy allegiance to the middle of the sixteenth century in Italian – and Spanish – painting. This proto-Baroque reaction against the overly intellectual, allegorical and anti-naturalistic complexities of Mannerist art has been called, logically enough, Anti-Mannerism. While the details and course of that reaction were early described (W. Friedlander, 1930) in 'mainstream' Italian painting, to my knowledge, later-sixteenth-century Spanish painting has not been treated as such, although such a thesis clarifies and re-evaluates both the significance of the period in itself and its place within national traditions.

In its Italian phase, Anti-Mannerism may be thought of, properly, as a 'neo-Renaissance' movement but such a description would not altogether apply in the case of Spain, granted our arguments to the effect that the essence of classicism never really took root there. Nevertheless, both Italian and Spanish Anti-Mannerism have formal qualities in common: spatial balance, monumental compactness, clarity of composition, harmony and assimilation of figures in near space, emphasis on corporeal elements, immediate understandability of composition and subject matter, an anti-linear return to the warmth of Venetian 'painterly' chiaroscuro, normative colour and dense weighty use of pigments.

In content, the reaction based upon objectivity and practical work, eschewing abstract theory, strove for a down-to-earth actuality and simplicity based upon truth to nature. These tendencies, in comparison with Mannerism, become most clear in the treatment of the transcendental: the ecstatic and the visionary are stated in direct, human terms. Mannerist affectations are either forgotten or abandoned and there is a suppression of the symbolic and the arcane. Even miracles are 'secularized' and are treated in a manner which moves from the moderately idealized to the crassly naturalistic. Like classical antiquity and the High Renaissance, Anti-Mannerism sees in the supernatural only a heightened form of human experience.

All of this is wrapped up, in large part, in the greater fabric of sixteenth-century religious reform movements. Early Spanish spokesmen openly advocated religious reform; for example, the twin brothers Alfonso and Juan de Valdés, the latter an important figure in the papal court of Hadrian VI, and both authors of the exquisitely written *Dialogues*. Further, during the Siege of Rome in 1527, a number of Spanish clerics had been pressing for a 'proto-Reformation' based upon an intensification of individual faith and the critical reading and revision of the Scriptures into Castilian. And it was, of course, the Spaniard Ignatius of Loyola who founded the Jesuit Order, spearhead of the militant Counter-Reformation.

During the Council of Trent (1545–63), in which the Spanish clergy exercised a major role, rulings were made in reference to the aims of art which advocated the return to more traditional forms; art was to be moral and didactic in purpose, and clarity in subject matter, classical decorum and dramatic or pathetic effects were to be encouraged. Works of art were to be, henceforth, 'salutary examples set before the eyes of the faithful'. Thus '[Mannerist] pictures with obscure and difficult meanings' were considered anathema as art was given a populist and non-aristocratic bent; paintings, in this sense, were 'used mostly as books for the illiterate'. This quotation and the following, from Bishop Paleotti's *Discourse on Sacred and Profane Images* (1582), make clear the ecclesiastic impetus given the painterly reformation: 'The good painter must . . . use a manner . . . expressing the necessary particulars and thereby avoiding misunderstandings or any ambiguous figures, as much as possible . . . Sometimes one tries to express things which by their nature cannot be expressed [in painting] . . . the safest remedy in this difficulty is to abstain from such subjects as much as possible.' It seems logical to expect that an intensely Catholic Spain would be quick (if not the first) to heed those clearly stated admonitions.

In another mode, *Don Quixote*, in its literary iconoclasm, might be called the great Anti-Mannerist novel but it too had its antecedents, such as the anonymous *Lazarillo de Tormes* (1554), and, of course, the exquisitely bare and intense writings of Luis de León and Sta Teresa of Ávila. What then is the evidence for this reforming and revitalizing movement within Spanish painting itself?

The genesis and spread of Anti-Mannerism in Spain was neither consistent nor universal. The Fleming, Pedro de Campaña (Pieter Kempeneer, 1503–80), like the Italian Savoldo, intermingles Mannerist and proto-Baroque tendencies. A leader of the emerging Sevillian School, his 'Hispanization' is shown in the *Descent from the Cross* (1547) in the manner of earthen colorations and Andalusian facial types. Compared with Machuca's work, Campaña's composition is clearly more inclined towards the classical mode of sturdy, equilateral triangular composition. In his later *Adoration of the Shepherds* (1557) a warm humanization is noted along with a firm, credible spatial sense. Another Sevillian, Luis de Vargas (1506–68), treats similar subject matter (1555) in a manner both tenderly characterized and monumental, although the figure groupings tend towards crowding. It is worth noting that this selfsame Sevillian School was, in the seventeenth century, to produce Velásquez and Murillo, among others; it is my contention that their Baroque warmth, naturalism and humanity were clearly anticipated in their less well known predecessors. On the other hand, one might choose to see such learnings emerging in the later Valencían School, as in the work of Juan de Juanes already discussed.

The deaf Juan Fernández de Navarrete (1526–79), 'el Mudo',

Pedro de Campaña *Descent from the Cross*. Panel, *c.* 1547. Cathedral, Seville.

Pedro de Campaña (attr.) *The Adoration of the Shepherds*. Panel, *c.* 1557. Church of Santa Ana, Seville.

Luis de Vargas *The Birth of Christ*. Panel, central section of the main altarpiece, *c.* 1555. Cathedral, Seville.

was one of several artists associated with the decoration of the Escorial. He is one of the earliest Spaniards to depend upon those Venetian painterly techniques which employed colourism and distant, atmospheric effects. His 1571 *Martyrdom of St James* makes an interesting counterpart to El Greco's rejected *St Maurice* by its cruel concentration upon *essential* action. His Corresgesque *Adoration* of 1575, on the other hand, shows a striking simplicity of essentially pictorial effect quite distinct from his colleague in the Escorial Gaspar Becerra's Michelangelesque – and late mannerist, *à la* School of Fontainebleau – frescoes in the Pardo Palace of *c*. 1565. Blas del Prado (*c*. 1545–1600), in his *Virgin and Child*, shows a conspicuous return to the calm Renaissance classicism of Fra Bartolomeo, in 1589. Thus one sees, after a lapse of some seventy years, a clearly deliberate revival of monumentality created through simple symmetrical compositions, uncomplicated sweeping drapery and psychological tranquillity. Alonso Sánchez Coello's *St Sebastian* executed in 1582, six years before his death, parallels the Italian Anti-Mannerist emphasis upon clear balanced compositions, set in an ample landscape, and credibility of pose and gesture. It should be pointed out, however, that this is rather different from the directions of his 'mannered' court portraiture.

On this note we take leave of the Anti-Mannerist movement in Spain which has been discussed at some length in order that we be better prepared to understand Ribalta and Ribera and the subsequent development of Baroque painting in Spain. The above should demonstrate that the art of Ribalta and Ribera has clear predecessors in intent and mood, if not precisely in style, and that one need not exclusively look to Italian sources (particularly Caravaggio) to explain their advent. Thus, Early Baroque Spanish painters are, in effect, concretizing already clearly expressed Spanish desires, manifested – as has been pointed out – in many ways, and which possibly even antedate Italian moves towards an art based upon unaffected naturalism and clarity of expression.

Juan Fernández de Navarrete ('El Mudo') *Martyrdom of St James.* Oil on canvas, *c.* 1571. Escorial.

Gaspar Becerra, detail of the fresco cycle from the ceiling of the Pardo Palace (Madrid), *c.* 1563. *in situ*.

Blas del Prado *Virgin and Child, with the Holy Family, St Ildefonso, St John the Evangelist, and the donor Alonso de Villegas.* Oil on canvas, *c.* 1589. Museo del Prado, Madrid.

Alonso Sánchez Coello *St Sebastian flanked by Saints Bernard and Francis.* Panel,
c. 1582. Museo del Prado, Madrid.

5 The 'National Style' and the Baroque

Antonio Palomino – in his *El museo pictórico y escala óptica* (1724), a pioneering attempt to emulate Vasari's history of Italian art and artists – cites the generation of artists born in the second half of the sixteenth century as the creators of an *estilo nacional* – a national style or expression – and equates this with an *estilo desornamentado* – essentially an 'unaffected naturalism'. In 1605, Cervantes, in the prologue to *Don Quixote*, had clearly stated the by then effective tenets of the national aesthetic: 'One has only to take advantage of imitation . . . the more perfect be that, the better one will write . . . Strive for the plain and simple with meaningful, honest and well-placed words . . . [thereby] painting, through the means of all that is graspable and palpable, one's intention to make concepts comprehensible without complicating or obscuring them.'

The Sevillian Francisco Pacheco's influential *El arte de la pintura* (1649), which reveals him to be a true follower of the Tridentine rulings, stated that 'the ends of painting, in general, will be, by means of imitation, to represent a given subject with all the power and propriety possible . . . the principle goal [of the artist] will be to achieve a state of grace through the study and practice of this profession'. Pacheco's painting, though not particularly significant in itself, stresses plastic form and verisimilitude in order to express his essentially unmaterialistic and quasi-mystical directions. He early fixed the iconography of the Immaculate Conception which was, however, to be given its greatest popularity by Murillo.

The revival of realism, and the 'National Style', received major expression in the work of Francisco Ribalta (1565–1628) who is essentially a member of the Madrid School and probably studied with Navarrete, el Mudo. Of his earlier works little remains but the development of his art may be said to be a long and rather difficult

Francisco Pacheco *The Immaculate Conception.* Oil on canvas, *c.* 1620. Cathedral, Seville.

Francisco Ribalta *St Bernard embracing Christ.* Oil on canvas, *c.* 1620–28. Museo del Prado, Madrid.

struggle against Mannerism. His later *St Bernard embracing Christ*, in the Prado, shows his eventual success in eradicating obscurantist affectations. Its mood, like that of his *Vision of St Francis*, is particularly direct and effective; here the significant truth of the human psychology, which underlies religious ecstasy, is stressed through simple gestures and unaffected spiritual communication. The desired effect is further enhanced, compositionally, by plain, monumental forms comfortably set in dramatic tenebrist lighting (*not*, we may assume, derived from Caravaggio). Ribalta's naturalism makes an interesting comparison to Machuca's agitated work of a hundred years earlier.

The Sevillian Juan de Roelas (*c.* 1560–1625), sometimes known as the Spanish Veronese, is to be noted for his dramatic, large and harmoniously composed scenes tied together by a controlled use of colour and an *estilo vaporoso* (luminous manner), which anticipates Murillo as do his genre types. Cited by Palomino as a major innovator of the 'unornamented' style, Francisco Herrera the Elder (*c.* 1590–1656) exhibits in the Prado *St Bonaventura received into the Franciscan Order* the typically Spanish taste for the anticlassical – manifested in the direct and passionate focus on the individual character of the subject – which, for clarity's sake, may be called a sort of 'impressionistic naturalism'.

The high water-mark of the strong 'quietistic' directions within the Spanish Baroque is to be seen in Francisco de Zurbarán (1598–1664). Born in Extremadura, he was to spend most of his life in Seville, although he died in Madrid. His art is best described as 'monastic' and serves as a documentary, almost eyewitness, record – employing Spanish veracity and earnestness – of the solitude and inwardly directed spiritual passion of the secluded monasteries. His particular intentions are revealed in the *Spiritual Guide* of Miguel de Molinos (1675) in which one reads that 'the soul gains more in . . . prayer, in complete withdrawal of the senses, and in mental power . . . than [through] penitent exercises, disciplines, etc. All this punishes only the *body*, but by withdrawal the *soul* is purified.'

Zurbarán is another, like El Greco, whose fame suffered an

Francisco Ribalta *Vision of St Francis*. Oil on canvas, *c.* 1625. Museo del Prado, Madrid.

Juan de Roelas *The Martyrdom of St Andrew*. Oil on canvas, *c.* 1609–13. Provincial Museum, Seville.

Francisco Herrera the Elder *St Bonaventura received into the Franciscan Order.*
c. 1628. Museo del Prado, Madrid.

eclipse until this century; however, Zurbarán has been revived
for very different reasons; namely, for his extreme concentration
upon *tangible* form which almost verges on the surreal. Palomino

Francisco de Zurbarán *The Vision of the Beato Alonso Rodríguez*. Oil on canvas, *c.* 1630. Academy of San Fernando, Madrid.

had said of his work 'all who see it and do not know it is a painting believe it to be a work of sculpture'; as such, it is of interest to compare him with the sculptor Pedro de Mena (1628–88) whose work

Francisco de Zurbarán *St Serapion*. Oil on canvas, *c.* 1628. Wadsworth Atheneum, Hartford (Conn.).

does look like that of Zurbarán. Such simultaneous vision gives further evidence of a homogeneity of aim in the arts of Spain for which it is difficult to find parallels.

Pedro de Mena *St Francis of Assisi*. Wood sculpture, 1663. Cathedral, Toledo.

Francisco de Zurbarán *Virgin and Child*. Oil on canvas, *c.* 1662. Museum, Bilbao.

While his figures in themselves are extremely 'statuesque' he, like his predecessors, relies upon abstract colour patterns and two-dimensionality of background (achieved, in this case, through the use of multiple vanishing points). The 'unreal' spatial mood of the environment is another way of expressing the transitory nature of this world which, in this sense, is but a temporary abode. In his later years he unfortunately found it necessary to try to emulate the extremely popular types and *estilo vaporoso* of Murillo, whose art is, in general, the stylistic and thematic antithesis of the quiet austerity of Zurbarán.

The manner in which the Spaniard was able to inject an intensity of expression into material objects, characteristic in themselves of his innate sense of ascetic idealism, is eloquently illustrated by the still-life compositions of Juan Sánchez-Cotán (1561–1627), which

Juan Sánchez-Cotán *Still Life*. Oil on canvas, *c.* 1602. Fine Arts Gallery, San Diego, California.

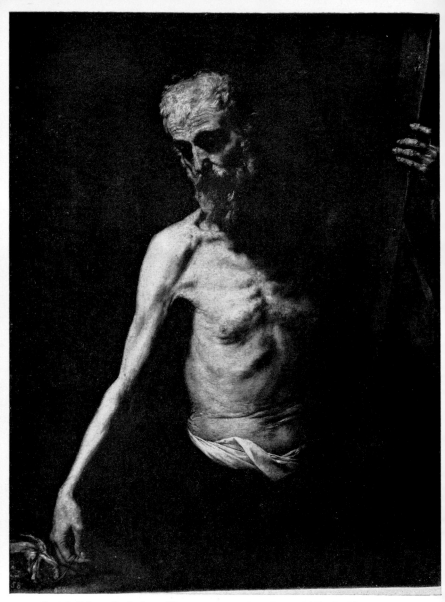

José de Ribera *St Andrew*. Oil on canvas, *c.* 1641. Museo del Prado, Madrid.

parallel Zurbarán in their concentration upon the tangible. These *bodegones* (still-lifes) seem like exercises in plane and solid geometry, constructed upon principles of musical harmony. It is worth noting here the Spanish popularity of, for instance, Archimedes' *Opera non nulla* (in the 1558 Venetian edition); after the founding of the Academy of Mathematics (1582) by the architect of the Escorial, Juan de Herrera, the purity of abstract (and 'platonic') geometry and arithmetic became all the rage.

If we have investigated some of the possibilities for sobriety and rationality within Baroque expression, we must not forget its other aspect of unbridled ecstasy and melodrama which, to many, seems more descriptive of the 'Baroque'. But we should point out that – in comparison with other European seventeenth-century art – the Spanish interpretation of the term is often most *un*-Baroque.

José de Ribera, 'il Spagnuoletto' (1591–1652), was noted, by his countrymen, for the impact he made upon Italian art which reversed the normal flow of influences; that notable turnabout certainly indicates the appropriateness of certain directions within the Spanish temperament to Baroque taste. It could be asserted that the general European mood of the seventeenth century was to be the key which finally unlocked Spanish genius and which enabled it to rise above its former provincial status. Born in Játiva (Valencia), Ribera studied in the provincial capital although not, apparently, with Ribalta. When he was around twenty, he went to Italy and, some ten years later, he settled in Naples where he died about forty years later after enjoying much fame and many honours in his adopted country. However, it should be recalled that Naples was then a Spanish possession – and had been since 1442 – and was ruled by Spanish viceroys; in effect, Ribera had chosen to settle in Phillip IV's easternmost province. His influence was to leave a lasting mark upon Neopolitan painting and Italian Baroque art.

In Ribera's work, one sees the full Baroque synthesis of the terrestrial and the supernatural, naturalism being the tangible vehicle by which mystic revelation is expressed. Ribera's concentration upon the experience of the individual – as opposed to an archetype – is a uniquely Spanish contribution; the psychology of

José de Ribera *Martyrdom of St Bartholomew*. Oil on canvas, *c*. 1630. Museo del Prado, Madrid.

the ideals of an often painful asceticism and solitary meditation is realized through a system based upon personal particulars. His actual technique – compared, in particular, with that of Zurbáran – is much more 'painterly'. Ribera painted quickly, in the *alla prima* manner, not allowing for each separate coat of pigment to dry. He employed a 'loaded brush' which created a corrugated, extremely tactile surface which, in a direct – and almost sculptural – fashion, is the pictorial equivalent of the dried, cracked skin of the world-weary and the aged or the lines of agony and suffering of the martyred. Compositionally, he strove to suppress irrelevancies by concentrating the action, by reducing backgrounds to a stage-like minimum and by employing light in a spotlight-like focus.

Jusepe Martínez, in his *Discursos practicables del noblísimo arte de la pintura* (*c*. 1675), lauded Ribera as 'a close imitator of nature'. This is brought out particularly in his treatment of mythological subjects, *de rigueur* in Italian art: as a Spaniard, however, he was wont to treat the Olympians and other Antique subjects with a rather disrespectful, mock realism. Such an approach is characteristic certainly of Velásquez as well as of most of his compatriots. For example Ribera's *Archimedes* treats the mathematician as though he were a beggar snatched from the teeming alleys of the Neopolitan seaport. This Hispanic – almost picaresque – realism, usually directly taken from life and based upon a keen sympathy for the individual, no matter what his particular foibles or disfigurations, is the keynote for his *Boy with a Clubfoot*.

Here it is worth while to discuss briefly the stylistic changes within his painting for they demonstrate how he and his peninsular contemporaries echo, in general, the different periods or generations within the larger development of the Baroque style. From 1620 to 1635 he employed a harsh tenebrist style. The next five years saw a lighter, more transparent use of colour and his brushwork became gentler and suaver. From 1640 to 1655, his modelling became yet more fluid and individual details were relinquished in favour of monumental effects. Subject matter is calmer and lighter in mood and the colour silvery and vaporous. These formal mutations correspond to those associated with the Early, High and Late Baroque styles.

The work of Diego de Velásquez (1588–1660) is the high water-mark of Spanish painting. Although his strict contemporary is Zurbarán, Velásquez was quite a different sort of person: a born aristocrat, worldly, well educated and eventually the intimate associate of rulers and pontiffs. And yet between the two – the

José de Ribera *Archimedes*. Oil on canvas, *c.* 1630. Prado, Madrid.

José de Ribera *Boy with a Clubfoot*. Oil on canvas, *c.* 1652. Musée du Louvre, Paris.

court favourite and the provincial monastic – one finds, for all their formal and social differences, a close spiritual kinship: the common national heritage of an anti-idealistic and anti-platonic emphasis on individual dignity and contemplative sobriety of expression. Further, they both exemplify that democratic quality (not especially in the strict political sense) which is a hallmark of Spanish society: the Spaniard feels that he can address either King or Christ on completely intimate and direct terms. It is this un-affected empathy and projection which has made the artificial and 'unreal' distance imposed by the canons of idealized art so difficult for him to understand.

Velásquez' parents, originally from Portugal, had settled in Seville. At the age of eleven, possibly after a brief apprenticeship with Herrera the Elder, he moved to the studio of Francisco Pacheco, who was later to become his father-in-law. Here he was introduced into a learned artistic circle – a quasi-Academy – and so became thoroughly conversant with current artistic theory and humanistic thought. His biographer, Antonio Palomino, noted Velásquez' studious preparations: 'He read Alberto Dürer on the proportions of the human body; Andrea Vesalius on anatomy; Giovanni Battista Porta on physiognomy; Daniele Barbaro on perspective; Euclid on geometry; Moya on arithmetic; Vitruvius, Vignola, and other authors on architecture. Like a bee, he carefully selected what suited his needs and would benefit posterity. On the nobility of painting he looked at the treatise of Romano Alberti . . . [and] he worked out his *idea della bellezza* with the help of Federico Zuccaro . . . Vasari inspired him with his *Lives of Famous Painters* and Borghini's *Il Riposo* described how to be a learned painter. He completed his education by reading the Bible and ancient classics and other important things, thus fertilizing his mind with erudition and wide knowledge of the arts . . .' Velásquez, therefore, was not (merely) an incomparable technician or, if you will, a superb optic nerve but was also – and always – a profound thinker.

His early period, 1617–23, is a Caravaggesque one, as seen in genre studies such as *The Water Carrier of Seville*; or, in religious

Diego de Velásquez *The Water Carrier of Seville*. Oil on canvas, *c.* 1619. Wellington Museum, London.

Diego de Velásquez *Adoration of the Magi*. Oil on canvas, *c.* 1617. Museo del **Prado**, Madrid.

matters, the handsome *Adoration of the Magi*. In the Spring of 1623 Velásquez was given an opportunity which was to change the course of his career from that of a painter of Seville into a painter for the world. A fellow Sevillian, the Royal Minister, the Count-Duke of Olivares, secured a court appointment for the talented youth and so he made the acquaintance of the then nineteen-year-old Phillip IV who was to be his lifelong friend and protector. Velásquez' star was set on its course.

An interesting work from this earlier period is the equestrian portrait of the Count-Duke, based, in general, upon Titian's mounted Charles V (in the Prado) and, ultimately, upon the famous Roman bronze statue of Marcus Aurelius. However, the artist was obliged to adopt a difficult and oblique pose in order to disguise the Minister's notorious obesity. In his sympathetic treatment of the court fools: dwarfs and buffoons – amusement devices unique to the Spanish court – he shows, on the other hand, an impressive ability to capture likeness, mood and movement. His lengthy series of 'normal' portraits, while obviously indebted to tradition, carry that genre to unexpected heights.

The celebrated *Triumph of Bacchus* (*Los Borrachos*) testifies to his lifelong, almost sceptical, attitude towards mythology which trait, as we have seen, is rooted in Spanish tradition. At this stage, the modelling is still more sculptural than painterly. But later works, such as the pensive *Mars* (*c.* 1642) and the pathos of *Mercury and Argos* (*c.* 1659) show, for all their technical differences, that the interpretation was to change little and that mythology remains another adjunct to unidealistic, but normative, psychological veracity and optical realism.

In late 1628 Rubens arrived in Madrid on a diplomatic mission and Velásquez shared his studio for eight months. The Fleming encouraged the younger Sevillian to broaden his cultural and artistic horizons and so, in order to advance himself, Velásquez set out upon a lengthy travelling apprenticeship in Italy. There, from 1629 to 1631, he familiarized himself with the expansive Venetian painterly manner and the Roman sense of harmonious and varied figure composition.

Diego de Velásquez *Phillip IV*. Oil on canvas, *c*. 1628. Museo del Prado, Madrid.

Diego de Velásquez *Equestrian Portrait of Don Gaspar Guzmán, Count Duke of Olivares*. Oil on canvas, *c.* 1633. Museo del Prado, Madrid.

Diego de Velásquez *The Court Buffoon Cabecillas* (*El Bobo de Coria*). Oil on canvas, *c*. 1640. Museo del Prado, Madrid.

Diego de Velásquez *Lady with a Fan* (*Francisca de Velásquez ?*). Oil on canvas,
c. 1640. Wallace Collection, London.

Diego de Velásquez *The Triumph of Bacchus*. Oil on canvas, *c.* 1644. Museo del Prado, Madrid.

Diego de Velásquez *Mercury and Argos*. Oil on canvas, *c.* 1659. Museo del Prado, Madrid.

Two years after his return he executed *The Surrender of Breda* (*Las Lanzas*) which synthesizes what he had learned abroad. It deals with the surrender, in 1625, of the Dutch city of Breda in a courtly, dignified, graceful and spectacular fashion. The action concentrates upon the ceremonious chivalry of the victorious Spanish commander, the Genoese general Ambrogio Spinola, in his gracious acceptance of the keys of the fortress from the defeated Justin of Nassau. However, there is here also a subtly disguised allegorical content which is often overlooked: the poses of the central grouping were based upon a little-known sixteenth-century print (after Marten de Vos) of Abraham and Melchisedek in which

Diego de Velásquez *The Surrender of Breda* (*Las Lanzas*). Oil on canvas, *c.* 1638. Museo del Prado, Madrid.

the latter offered bread and wine to the victorious and generous-spirited Abraham. Thus Velásquez, in his deliberate choice of that composition, implied that the Spanish victory, like Abraham's, was due to heavenly aid and that this, in turn, demanded that a Christian generosity be extended to the defeated. One could discuss the element of characterization achieved by purely formal means at great length but suffice it here to point out the disciplined bank of Spanish lances and the calm, compact ranks of the victors, neatly boxed by the *repoussoir* device of the horse, which contrast with the irregular silhouettes of the loosely composed and spottily lit knot of Dutchmen. Surely this is one of the most impressive works ever committed to canvas.

Certainly, the Prado *Maids of Honour* (*Las Meninas*) also functions as an incredible *tour de force* and one could rest quite content with its almost incredible illusionistic effects. Yet we must rid ourselves of that notion, implanted by nineteenth-century 'impressionistic' art criticism, that Velásquez was merely an 'eye' which functioned in the efficient and thoughtless manner of the camera. I will pass briefly over the obviously superb composition: it is put together with a rigour of balance and sense of pattern which finds its peer in Mondrian. But I find it difficult to imagine who could equal that sense of palpable atmosphere and latent action which is so much Velásquez'. Certainly his ability to capture reality was astounding. In the next generation, Palomino gives valuable information on the manner in which he was able to achieve these effects: 'On occasion, he used long-handled brushes, which enabled him to paint at a distance from the canvas. Thus, when you look at it up close it is hard to see what is going on, but from a distance it is a miracle . . . The figure painting is superior, the conception new, and in short it is impossible to overrate this painting because *it is truth, not painting*.'

From the point of view of *idea*, one must note the significance of the intrusion of the artist, on the left side, picturing himself in the very act of capturing the scene on canvas. By so projecting himself, he has established a direct unity of thought and action, the 'stage' is set but also our attention is quietly drawn to the fact that it is the

Diego de Velásquez *The Maids of Honour* (*Las Meninas*). Oil on canvas, *c.* 1656. Museo del Prado, Madrid.

Diego de Velásquez *Self-Portrait*, detail from *Las Meninas*. Oil on canvas, *c.* 1656. Museo del Prado, Madrid.

conscious and deliberate act (idea) of a given person. Notice, too, that the artist is not depicted in the specific act of painting but is instead seen reflectively pondering upon the idea which will cause him to paint in a moment. Also, by his aristocratic pose and his intimate proximity to royalty, he underlines the idea of the nobility of painting and, by extension, that it is an act of the mind, before being of the hand: therefore painting is a liberal, rather than a mechanical, art. *Las Meninas* is perhaps the subtlest and most profoundly compact statement of the doctrine of *Ut Pictura Poësis* – the humanistic theory of art.

In the above we have merely scratched the surface of the variety and genius of Velásquez who appeals deeply to both the eye and the mind – it must not be forgotten that, to Velásquez, both were indivisible, a notion which we in our fragmented age may tend to overlook.

A suave Late Baroque style is the keynote of Bartolomé Esteban Murillo (1617–82), the (it appears) self-taught Sevillian master whom Rococo tastes of the eighteenth century, especially in England, valued higher than either Titian or Rubens. However, there were those in Spain who felt that he had abandoned the National Style: Palomino states that Murillo 'charms by sweetness and attractive beauty' but feels that in his recognition of 'the great seductive power of colour for winning popular favour', he was unfortunate in abandoning 'drawing, that excellence of all that is most refined and transcendental (and which) does *not* move the masses'. He ascribes Murillo's reliance upon the sensual aspect of colour and his popularity abroad to un-Spanish tastes as 'foreigners do not want to concede fame to any Spanish painter who has not passed through an Italian customshouse'. Further, his fame has suffered due, in part, to what Ortega y Gasset calls that 'dehumanization' of taste in this century which considers sentiments anathema and, further, to Protestant embarrassment before Catholic ecstasy.

Murillo's style, which he formed without ever leaving Seville, quickly moved from Early Baroque tenebrism to *vaporoso* luminism. In his many *Immaculatas* he created a classic type. One might contrast the different approaches to religious imagery – Murillo's on the one hand and Zurbarán's on the other – by again citing Padre Molino's *Spiritual Guide* in which he pointed out that 'there are two ways of praying – tenderly, fondly, lovingly and full of feeling – or humbly, dryly, comfortless and darkly'.

However, perhaps it is his genre studies that best exhibit his pungent and actually quite fresh psychological acumen. His democratic sense is best appreciated here and, in fact, he was a master of the nonconformist, anti-heroic scene in which the people – *el pueblo* – is the central protagonist. While taste will always obey the vicissitudes of time and fashion, the delightful freshness and vivacity of his sensuous paint surfaces remain constant.

Bartolomé Esteban Murillo *Girls at a Window*. Oil on canvas, *c.* 1665. National Gallery, Washington, DC.

Bartolomé Esteban Murillo *The Aranjuez Immaculata*. Oil on canvas, *c.* 1650–60. Museo del Prado, Madrid.

6 *The Rococo, Goya and After*

In 1701 Phillip of Anjou was proclaimed King Felipe V and the throne passed to the French house of Bourbon. The next year saw the beginning of the War of the Spanish Succession, lasting until 1713 and the Peace of Utrecht, in which Spain lost most of her European possessions, including Gibraltar. The eighteenth century was a period of humiliation, waning political power and privation. It was also a period of a pitiful decline in the arts as the native traits of Spanish culture gave way under foreign influences. Simplicity and veracity were, in the main, abandoned in favour of Rococo complexity, artifice and frivolity. The many foreign artists invited by the Bourbon court – Mengs, Tiepolo, Juvarra, Houasse,

Luis Meléndez *Still Life*. Oil on canvas, 1772. Museo del Prado, Madrid.

Luis Paret *Charles III Dining Before his Court*. Panel, *c*. 1775. Museo del Prado, Madrid.

Van Loo, Ranc, etc. – forced native talent to go, as it were, 'underground'.

Luis Meléndez (1716–80), sometimes called the 'Spanish Chardin', is noted for his many *bodegones*. However, these still-life studies, in comparison with those of Sánchez-Cotán or Zurbarán, show – for all their obvious charm – a certain relaxation of concentration and a general lightening of mood. Although a contemporary of Goya, Luis Paret y Alcázar (1746–99) seems a later (and weaker) follower of Watteau. Paret was eventually banished (for his romantic entanglements) to Puerto Rico and so became the only significant European artist in Spanish America in that century. Francisco

125

Francisco Bayeu *Olympus: The Battle of the Gods.* Study for a fresco in the Royal Palace, Madrid. Oil on canvas, *c.* 1790. Museo del Prado, Madrid.

Bayeu (1734–95), Goya's teacher and father-in-law, executed frescoes in the airy manner of Tiepolo.

Against this somewhat sorry backdrop of foreign domination and national debilitation, the art of Francisco de Goya y Lucientes (1746–1828) seems astonishing. Briefly, the best way to understand this phenomenon is to consider him as the delayed reaffirmation of the Spanish ideals of spontaneous, direct expression and ethical naturalism. This latter term perhaps deserves further explanation: 'realism' is a specific *technique* which intends to capture what one sees with the utmost optical fidelity; 'naturalism' is an *attitude* which seeks to capture life as it is without the distortions of idealism or other *a priori* impositions. Suffice it to say that Goya was an artist who, particularly in his expressionistic later works, transcended realism in order to fix his naturalistic commitment (hence, ethical sense) to the disillusioning world around him. By his attachment to social comment and commitment, he returned to that native tradition which considers painting as a vehicle for ideas as opposed to the concept of painting for art's sake.

Goya was born in Zaragoza (Aragón) and was in Madrid by 1766 (his reasons for leaving – and other aspects of his life – have been distorted by a great deal of romantic poppycock); by 1771 he was in Rome and so became cognizant of the latest trends in painting abroad. Having returned to Madrid in 1775 he began, a year later, to produce cartoons for the rejuvenated Royal Tapestry Factory, embarking on a career which, like that of Velásquez, was to bring him great success: he was appointed *primer pintor de cámara* (Principal Painter to the King) in 1799 and was well known and appreciated by his contemporaries. But earlier, in 1792, due to an unknown illness he, like Beethoven, became deaf and introspective. This was probably instrumental in causing him to, as a contemporary noted, 'make observations for which commissioned works generally have no room, and in which fantasy and invention have no limit'. But, in the broader sense, Goya's art is a microcosmic vision of the collapse of the utopian optimism of the Age of Reason and Enlightenment earlier foreshadowed in Alexander Pope's problematic query: 'With terrors round, can reason hold her throne, / Despite the known, nor tremble at the unknown? / Survey both worlds, intrepid and entire, / In spite of witches, devils, dreams and fire?' Goya's outraged *The Sleep of Reason Produces Monsters* almost seems an illustration to the above.

But Goya's early works, the painted tapestry designs (a total of sixty-six over a period of fifteen years), concern themselves with a delight in people and their diversions; they are, for the most part, full of a *joie de vivre* that reflects the hermetic Bourbon view of the bucolic life enjoyed by their Spanish subjects. However the native quality comes through: in the clothing and manners; in the earthen colour; and, later in the series, in occasional glimpses of pain and hardship, as seen in *Winter* and *The Wounded Mason*. Goya seems to have picked up from the exigencies of the weaving medium certain stylistic traits which he was not to relinquish: a general sketchiness, schematized colour areas, simple silhouettes in chiaroscuro, diaphanous backgrounds and essential action

Francisco Goya *The Sleep of Reason Produces Monsters*, study for No 43 of *Los Caprichos*, c. 1797. Museo del Prado, Madrid.

Francisco Goya *The Wounded Mason*. Tapestry cartoon, *c.* 1786. Museo del Prado, Madrid.

suppressing irrelevant details. His technique was to prepare his canvas with a warm undercoat which, for not being completely covered with subsequent coats, lent a hot, earthy tonality to the whole; he would then employ sweeping, liquid brushstrokes and would apply the pigment with palette knife, a wide spatula, a sponge or even with his fingers. His style might be considered somewhat 'impressionistic' in as much as he strove – obsessed by the inherent drama of light and shadow – to capture visual rather than structural phenomena. In general, he did not find 'finish' congenial to his purposes and, apparently, he worked without any preparatory sketches and did not later modify his canvases

Francisco Goya *The Parasol*. Tapestry cartoon, *c*. 1777. Museo del Prado, Madrid.

(conversely, one can discern many corrections in Velásquez' work indicating the latter's precise approach).

Goya's major portraits are of the highest interest as they show a new emphasis upon psychology over physiology. While there is a complete lack of idealization, nevertheless, they are not ironic or satirical in intention – as some critics wrongly assume, especially when confronted with the unheroic, *bourgeois* banality of *The Family of Charles IV* – rather they culminate the Spanish predilection for accepting things and people 'as they are'. Sometimes, however, especially in his depictions of women, Goya conveys a sense of expectation and mystery that is quite bewitching – and

Francisco Goya *The Family of Charles IV*. Oil on canvas, *c*. 1800. Museo del Prado, Madrid.

Francisco Goya *The Second of May, 1808: the Battle with the Mamelukes in Madrid.*
Oil on canvas, *c.* 1814. Museo del Prado, Madrid.

quite distant from the brilliantly executed and vivacious repre-
sentations of, say, a Gainsborough or a Reynolds. Interesting, too,
is the fact that even at the height of his popularity and prestige,
Goya seemed, to academic circles, the incarnation of anti-art and
anti-culture and yet, in a uniquely Spanish manner, his works were
widely admired precisely because they were not understood!

Like Beethoven, Goya had originally been an admirer of
Napoleon. But in 1808 the Spanish 'War of Independence' suddenly
began as the people of Madrid spontaneously rose against the
oppressive French mercenaries occupying the capital, thereby

Francisco Goya *Doña María del Pilar Teresa Cayetana Álvarez de Toledo, The
Duchess of Alba.* Oil on canvas, *c.* 1795. Duke of Alba Collection, Madrid.

unleashing six years of primitive passions and bloody guerrilla warfare. Goya, profoundly moved and horrified by this ultimate 'sleep of reason', composed his brutal series of etchings, the *Disasters of War*, the first – and probably unsurpassable – universal anti-war statement in art. Some time after 1808 he painted the frighteningly enigmatic *Colossos*, an almost surrealistic – perhaps in current psychological jargon 'sublimated' – depiction of panic and mass terror. It is this sense of unfocused horror and general nightmare which was the impulsive force behind the truly titanic terrors of the wall paintings of the *Villa of the Deafman* (*Quinta del Sordo*) done some ten years later in his cottage outside Madrid, which truly deserve the appellation 'expressionistic'. These 'black paintings' (*pinturas negras*) are not true frescoes but are rather

Francisco Goya *Rightly or Wrongly*. Etching from the *Disasters of War*, before 1820. F. Torelló Collection, Barcelona.

Francisco Goya *The Colossos* (or *Panic*). Oil on canvas, *c*. 1808–12. Museo del Prado, Madrid.

oils directly and hastily applied to bare walls and were hardly intended for public exposure although, fortunately, they have been transferred to the Prado. These are best described as the sub-verbal soliloquies of one tortured by omnipresent visions of a world gone mad.

Francisco Goya *Saturn devouring his Children*. Oil painting from the walls of the *Quinta del Sordo*, c. 1820–22. Museo del Prado, Madrid.

Francisco Goya *The Duel with Clubs*. Oil painting from the walls of the *Quinta del Sordo*, 1820–22. Museo del Prado, Madrid.

Leonardo Alenza *Los Románticos!* Museum of Modern Art, Madrid.

Antonio Esquivel *A Reading by the Poet Zorrilla in the Painter's Studio*. Oil on canvas, *c*. 1842. Museum of Modern Art, Madrid.

After Goya, painting in nineteenth-century Spain seems rather tame; perhaps this is why it is, unfortunately, so little known beyond the Pyrenees although it often has a great deal of interest in its own right. The first half of the century shows a regressive tendency towards photographic accuracy and blandness of content expressive of bourgeois decorum. Evidence for an early Spanish aversion to the excesses of the Romantics is to be seen in the splendidly ironic *Los Románticos!* of Leonardo Alenza (1807–45) in which the impassioned emaciated figure, clad in a sort of toga, clutches at his breast about to stab himself while flinging himself off a precipice. The background contains the entire melodramatic

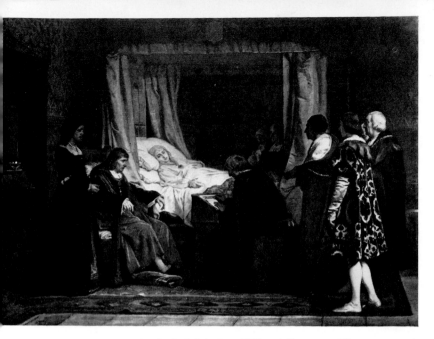

Eduardo Rosales *Isabella the Catholic's Last Will and Testament.* Oil on canvas, *c.* 1870. Museum of Modern Art, Madrid.

apparatus of Romantic scenography: stormy skies, barren land-scape, a tree with a hanged man and, on the rock itself, the poet's materials. But, for the most part, academic painting favoured, more so than in the rest of Europe, renderings of stoic political executions and large death-bed scenes.

In the second half of the century, *Costumbrismo* (the genre depiction of the native life and customs, also much evident in the literature of the period) is charmingly treated by the Catalan Mariano Fortuny (1838–74). Echoes of French impressionism are brilliantly adopted by Joaquín Sorolla (1863–1923) who is a master of light and sun. At the end of the century, the painting of Ignacio

Mariano Fortuny *The Vicarage*. Oil on canvas, *c.* 1870. Museum of Modern Art, Barcelona.

Joaquín Sorolla *After Bathing*. Oil on canvas, 1890 (?). Museum of Modern Art, Madrid.

Ignacio Zuloaga *El Cristo de la Sangre*. Oil on canvas, *c.* 1911. Museum of Modern Art, Madrid.

Zuloaga (1870–1945) marks a conscious attempt to return to the mainstream of Spanish tradition. His work is the major pictorial expression of the 'Generation of '98', whose members included writers, historians, philosophers and scientists of European magnitude: Ortega y Gasset, Unamuno, Menéndez-Pidal, etc., who sought – after the disillusioning Spanish–American War which finally ended the long (and mostly disastrous) Spanish Imperial Dream – to re-examine and reaffirm the autonomous essence of native character and tradition.

7　The Twentieth Century: a Sketch

At the turn of the century one finds the *noventaochentistas* intending to renew Spanish culture through a somewhat jaundiced and introspective autopsy of its traditions and spirit. At the same time another dynamic and progressive group were seeking to formulate a particularly 'modernistic' spirit to cope with the very altered and non-traditional world in which they found themselves. The major creative ferment was found in Barcelona, always more dynamic and centrifugally 'European' than dour and centralist Madrid. The outside world mainly knows of this Catalan creative fervour through the medium of the very visible and well known exercises in tectonics of the inspired architect Antonio Gaudí (1852–1926), but recent researches into this fascinating period, particularly by Professor Alexandre Cirici Pellicer, have uncovered a surprising store of buried *fin de siècle* wealth.

It is worth pointing out that the Catalans themselves felt that they were taking part in a *Renaixença* – a 'renaissance' not merely artistic but also musical, literary, industrial and political. Certainly, in purely formal terms, the main direction is that known as 'art nouveau', but behind the often sentimental neo-medievalisms and other historicist reversions lurks a tough, truly modern, attitude which asserts the autonomy of the artistic vision and gives the artist free rein to reconstruct visual appearances according to his own convictions. It was in this *milieu* of passionate aestheticism and formal disintegrations and reintegrations that the young Picasso took the first bold steps in his long career.

Pablo Ruiz y Picasso (b. 1881) was, however, of Andalusian origins; his family had resided in Málaga for some time. Perhaps the best way to get at the complex Picasso problem – *le mystère Picasso* – is to discuss him as an 'uprooted' sensibility. Just as in his formative youth he was never able to attach himself to any particular locale long enough to 'identify' with its very distinct historical, cultural and geographical situations – when he was ten, his family moved to the foggy Galician port of La Coruña and, four years later, they transported him to the very different bustling activity of industrial, class-torn, anarchistic Barcelona – so, too, in his mature years he has, unfortunately, often seemed unwilling to be more than a very clever, if somewhat negative, stylistic nomad. It is revealing that he himself has said: 'A painting is a sum of *destructions*.'

This brings up some points made by the late, excellently versatile scholar, Don Ramón Menéndez Pidal: that the haughty and exalted-minded Spaniard delights in a hermit-like detachment from the concerns of the material world. This trait, coupled with the other aspect of his arrogant self-confidence – sometimes to the point of non-participatory 'don't give a damn' – permits him, like Picasso, to exercise a complete disdain for the intrinsic significance of 'things' (and a style, in this sense, becomes a mere object to be utilized or wilfully manipulated) to the point of arbitrariness. Don Ramón characterizes the Spaniard as being alternately given to stoic apathy and frenetic energy: this, in the aesthetic field, leads him to have absolute confidence in the *premier coup*. Certainly, Picasso's large body of work betrays a credo of improvisation and rapid, copious production which, in its weaker moments, 'leads communally to an abandoned facility', pernicious practices which, due in part to his enormous prestige, have become *de rigueur* among the ranks of the *avant-garde*. While the above assertions may or may not always apply to Picasso's situation, one must agree with John Berger, in his brilliantly didactic and iconoclastic study of Picasso, when he states that 'after all, every Spaniard is different and yet every Spaniard is Spanish'.

Picasso has clearly demonstrated his disdain for rationality and the individual in his belief that the artist is merely the neutral, detached, conductor of incomprehensible and demonic creative energies: 'An artist works of necessity . . . he himself is only a trifling bit of the world . . . no more importance should be attached to him than to plenty of other things which please us in the world.' This is extraordinarily reminiscent of Seneca's admonition to remember that 'all things are equally unimportant, presenting a different appearance on the outside, but equally empty within!' Perhaps it was an awareness of this inner 'emptiness' that caused Picasso to speak of 'the several manners I have used' which he denies are 'an evolution or steps towards an unknown ideal of painting'. His uncommitted, anti-historical bias has also been

Pablo Picasso *The Abandoned*. Oil on canvas, 1902. Picasso Museum, Barcelona.

unequivocally admitted: 'When I have something to express, I have done it without thinking of the past or the present.'

We can now begin to discuss the various 'manners' of Picasso. He was initially caught up in the late nineteenth-century tourist-class excursions into the squalid life-styles of the *demi-mondaines*. His 'Blue' and 'Rose' period-exercises in proletarian pathos were influenced by the gypsy character-studies of Isidro Nonell (1873–1911) who used acid colours and broken brushwork to keynote psychological effects. It is notable that it is this earlier work of Picasso,

Isidro Nonell *Repose*. Oil on canvas, 1904. Museum of Modern Art, Barcelona.

with its very accessible sentimentality and attractively stated air of superficial social involvement which has proved extremely appealing to the wealthy collector-class. In fact, in 1964, a three- by two-foot gouache in this genre fetched some £80,000 (or nearly a quarter of a million dollars)!

From this earlier period, and throughout most of his career, he consciously and/or unconsciously – in spite of his usual avowed anti-historic attitudes – will return to various elements in traditional Spanish art: the jagged primitive vitality and simplified forms of Iberian art; the flat, austere, linear patterns of Romanesque painting; the harsh, detached observation of Medieval and Renaissance martyrdoms; the elongated, malleable forms of Gothic sculpture; the sinuous and elegant distortions of reality practised by the Mannerists; El Greco's colour discords; or even – on occasion – the monumentally undeviating vision of Zurbarán, Velásquez and Goya. One must bear in mind, therefore, that Picasso – like Spanish art itself – is extremely eclectic, although he seems to have chosen, for the most part, to forget its ethical basis.

In 1900 he visited Paris and returned three years later to take up permanent residence. Thus, like Ribera, he joined the long list of expatriate artists. The Bohemian, 'liberated', atmosphere of Paris eventually brought him out of his 'Harlequin' series and enabled him to evolve a 'classical' style based upon clarity of formal relations in which subjectivity and pretentiousness are reduced to a happy minimum. The decisive shift, under the dual impulses of post-Impressionism – Cézanne in particular – and the primitivism of Iberian and African sculpture, is clearly seen in the 1907 *Les Demoiselles d'Avignon* ('Avignon' in this case referring to an infamous street in Barcelona's red-light district). The subsequent evolution of Cubism was more than a mere stylistic reaction; it was a whole new vision of the concrete comparable in many ways to the change of mind demanded by the Renaissance.

The seeds of this viewpoint were sown by Courbet's defiant anti-'Art' materialism and by Cézanne's post-Realist rigorous investigations into the nature of natural appearances. The intention was revolutionary in that it overturned the seemingly

146

exhausted conventions of pictorial illusionism (chiaroscuro and perspective) to restore a positive, 'real' vision by applying a post-Marxist kind of dialectical materialism to art. It was also very 'modern' in its positive (if belated) acceptance of the modern world's un-'natural', un-'art-like', constructions; it accepted the man-made even to the lavish and unembarrassed use of the 'found object'. Also the fact that Cubism is so very austere and anti-sensual in its demands further served to make it congenial to the Spaniard: it is no accident that a major innovator and its most

Pablo Picasso *Les Demoiselles d'Avignon*, 1907. Museum of Modern Art, New York.

Juan Gris *Breakfast*. Mixed media, 1915. Museum of Modern Art, Paris.

consistently intellectual practitioner should be the Madrid-born
Juan Gris (1887–1927).

Picasso's art was posed a critical point by the universal catas-
trophe of the first world war. For the purposes of our argument, it
is extremely significant that he did *not* react, in any meaningful
way in his art, to the barbaric butchery that was going on barely
a few hundred miles away. His subsequent painting turned its
back upon the convulsed post-war world and he uncommittedly
returned to 'Art': style, elegance and draughtsmanship. While his
work up to 1935 is extremely handsome, exotic and most interesting
formally, it usually fails to touch the heart for want of anything
that could pass for a meaningful statement – apart from its hermetic
self. Also, Picasso's discussions on the history of art began at this
point: Ingres and Poussin, Titian and Velásquez, Delacroix and
Manet, and even Goya and Van Gogh become stylistic grist for his
art mill.

Pablo Picasso *Study after Velásquez: 'Las Meninas'*, 1957. Picasso Museum,
Barcelona.

In the works of this period Picasso shows himself to be the arch-Mannerist: forms are divorced from content and styles become mere drapery over a rather bare spiritual armature. A good example of his inability to communicate because of a prolix, and wholly inappropriate, grammar is seen in his rather ludicrous *Massacre in Korea* (1951) which purports to do for the oppressed (although rather distant in every way) Asians what *Guernica* did for his fellow-countrymen less than a decade and a half before. But he has by this stage become *too* sophisticated to accommodate himself comfortably to the desired effect of fierce outrage at mindless barbarism and cruelty. Yet he is here perhaps *too* unintellectual to realize the inherent absurdity of his use of stylization. He obviously wishes to make a clear statement and yet, for incomprehensible reasons, uses unnecessarily unclear means to do so. In short, while admittedly sophisticated and skilled as an optical technician, he has a not large enough stature as a humanist to achieve a meaningful and universally credible allegory as Goya might have done. The dislocation of sense and sensibility is obvious.

Another Spanish artist who has been 'blessed' (or cursed) with plentiful sycophantic success is the Catalan Salvador Dalí (b. 1904). Dalí, a curious admixture of showman, technician and all-round *enfant terrible*, although he began as a Cubist, has since graduated to High Priest of Surrealism. Lately, however, his creative imagination seems somewhat withered by his conversion from fervent Marxism to an equally fervent Catholicism; there are in this *volte-face* indications of ideological schizophrenia and there is also abundant evidence, in his work itself, of an inability to be consistently committed to meaningful ideals – of either a stylistic or a humanitarian sort. Perhaps this dilemma reflects the disjointed, 'invertebrate' character of Spanish society itself. Or, on the other hand, perhaps he, who above all others symbolizes 'Surrealism' to the collective public mind, is merely embarrassed by his abundant, although flawed, talents.

Dalí's occasionally miniaturist style – used to recapitulate endlessly his fantastic, neurotic and megalomaniacal childhood experiences – manifests his adulation of the precisions and cloacal colorations of nineteenth-century academicians of the ilk of Jean Millet, Arnold Böcklin and particularly Ernest Meissonier. His content is patently post-Freudian – with Italian *metafísica* and Picasso's neo-neo-classicisms for sauce. Dalí has even gone so far as to formulate a theoretical stance for his production which he amusingly labels 'paranoic-critical'. Perhaps embarrassingly revelatory of the pathological essence of his probable significance is the Tate canvas entitled *The Metamorphosis of Narcissus* (1937). In retrospect, none the less, I suggest that posterity will more warmly recall his cinematic collaboration with Luis Buñuel in *Un Chien Andalou* (1928) and *L'Age d'Or* (1930). 'Concrete' surrealism seems better suited to the film as the images pass so quickly that one does not have to dwell overlong upon them; too close scrutiny often reveals banality. While, in the historical sense, the traditional Spanish taste for the popular theatre suggests that *cine-drama* will be more congenial to and expressive of their tastes and strengths, cinema itself in Spain – up to this writing – is erratic, although often brilliant and overwhelming (e.g. Buñuel, Bardem, Saura, etc.).

Salvador Dalí *The Metamorphosis of Narcissus*. Oil on canvas, 1937. Tate Gallery, London.

The Catalan Joán Miró (b. 1893) is a master both of the surrealist idiom and of painting. In love with his native land, he has never felt the obligation to renounce Spanish tradition and mood; he builds upon it in a uniquely flexible manner. Miró's distortions are both meaningful and witty: his mordant humour and fantasy are presented with an absolutely deadpan straightforwardness that seems like *socarronería* (cunning) on canvas. One is impressed by his consistent dedication to and belief in his art regardless of his stylistic mutations, whereas Picasso and Dalí seem, at least to this writer, often to be merely 'manipulators', albeit endlessly clever

Joán Miró *The Garden* (*L'Hort*). 1918. National Museum, Estocolmo.

Joán Miró *Canvas* (*Lienzo*). Oil on canvas, 1953. Solomon Guggenheim Museum, New York.

and entertaining ones. Above all, it is a rare and pleasant experience to be confronted with an artist who can be unpretentiously charming without ever descending to the sentimental or the doctrinaire. Stylistically, Miró began in a Cézanne–Van Gogh vein, with vivid colour harmonies *à la* Matisse. He was also most appreciative of the naïve seriousness of Douanier Rousseau. He continued with a sort of geometric primitive realism until 1924, after which he moved into a unique and quite convincing, in its own terms, world of fantastic forms and situations. Some of his organic shapes are surprisingly – and not altogether fortuitously, one must suspect from his avowed pride in his Spanish heritage – reminiscent of Levantine cave paintings.

This sort of 'abstract' Surrealism – as best represented by Miró, André Masson and the Chilean Matta Echaurren – is variously known as 'organic', 'biomorphic', 'emblematic' or 'absolute', and it is, in artistic terms, a seemingly more convincing approach to the desired ends of revealing unconscious states through conscious reason than are Dalí's 'painted photographs'. In its liberation from the material and the concrete and in its veneration of the unfettered

153

response to media verging on *tachisme*, Miró's work sets an obvious precedent for Abstract Expressionism: he had been, for instance, a regular exhibitor in New York since 1930 and, as leader of the 'organic' surrealists, he made a profound impact on post-war American painters trying to emerge from the murky waters of 'Regionalism' and 'Social Realism'.

In Spain the murderous devastation of the Civil War, the strained post-war economy, and continued ideological repressions restrained progress in the arts for over a decade. That a thaw had finally begun, as the fifties were well under way, was signalled by the development of a 'School' of Barcelona (mainly, Antoni Tàpies (b. 1923), Modest Cuixart and Joán Josep Tharrats) and a somewhat later 'School' of Madrid (The 'El Paso' group of Antonio Saura (b. 1930), Rafael Canogar, Manolo Millarès, Luis Feito, etc.), although both seem rather indivisible in the larger sense. While most of these post-war artists have been abroad – obviously, the Spanish artist can no longer afford to be narrowly provincial – their main intention seems to be an ethical one of providing their somewhat anachronistic society with contemporary aesthetic values and experiences which should, at the same time, reflect tradition without being circumscribed by the sentimental, the antiquated or the chauvinistic.

This ethical and didactic intent – already noted as a persistent trait – is revealed by the many, almost evangelical, publications in which they have involved themselves and of which the early *Dau al Set* (*Seven-Spot Die*, in Catalan) is the most notable. While collectively their work can hardly be said to have enjoyed in Spain itself the esteem and success it has known elsewhere they have nevertheless renounced expatriation as they fully realize the danger faced by the modern artist who cuts himself off from his native environment and inspiration with a resultant debilitating effect on the creative imagination.

While determined to be 'modern' in the international sense, they have also tried hard to remain 'Spanish'. They have adapted a post-cubist sort of anti-Mannerism – through the specific means of *art informel* – in which they question ethically the established principles

Antonio Saura *Imaginary Portrait of Goya*, 1959–60. Pierre Matisse Gallery, New York.

of theoretical and doctrinaire compositional 'correctness'; illusionism as a thing in itself; and the enshrined priority of elegance and attractiveness over vigorously direct and untrammelled expression. They also insist upon truth to materials and refuse to deny the literal significance of objects and textures as things in themselves relying upon the totality and concreteness of the image as presented. A thick gritty texture becomes a wall encrusted with the *graffiti* of generations; a torn cloth, the ripped *traje de luces* of the martyred *matador*; earthy impastos become a microcosmic investigation of the underlying substance of the *pinturas negras*; dynamic paint swirls blossom like the unrestrained polychromed foliage of a baroque *retablo*.

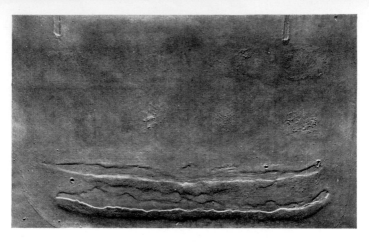

Antoni Tàpies *City Hall* (El Ayuntamiento). Oil on canvas. Museum of Modern Art, Barcelona.

Styles change: by the time we think we have grasped the shape and significance of the *avant garde*, we are already performing the post-mortem of the art historian. A post-tachisme reaction is discernible, in favour of a return to the specific, empirically 'identifiable' image: the younger Juan Genovés (b. 1930) uses the mass-produced photograph to make a chilling comment on the role of 'mass-man' as victim. The younger, rising painters demonstrate an ability to express the modern 'mood' in a sincere and meaningful way while retaining a uniquely national flavour, reflecting venerable native traditions and the continued vitality of the arts in Spain in spite of their many vicissitudes and erratic development, within the fluctuating and frenetic 'global village'. If the main problem facing the deracinated, aesthetically and stylistically confused 'Mid-Atlantic' artist is that of the heartless search for novelties, then that which now confronts the Spaniard is a more fundamental one: *Renovatio*.

Bibliography

This is a brief indication, for the interested student, of what I have found to be the more useful sources on the general subject; it is necessary to cite some works in Spanish as a great deal of valuable material has yet to be translated into English.

Ainaud, J. and W.W.S. Cook *Spain – Romanesque Paintings*. UNESCO 1957.

Arnason, H.H. *History of Modern Art*. New York 1968.

Arribas, A. *The Iberians*. London 1963.

Ars Hispaniae (various authors). 18 vols. Madrid 1947 *et seq.*

Berger, J. *The Success and Failure of Picasso*. Harmondsworth 1965.

Brenan, G. *The Literature of the Spanish People*. Cambridge 1951.

Brown, J. and R. Enggass *Sources and Documents in the History of Art: Italy and Spain, 1600–1750*. Englewood Cliffs (New Jersey) 1970.

Cirici Pellicer, A. *El Arte Modernística Catalán*. Barcelona 1951.

Cuttler, C.D. *Northern Painting: From Pucelle to Bruegel*. New York 1968.

Elliott, J.H. *Imperial Spain, 1469–1716*. New York 1963.

Friedländer, W. *Mannerism and Anti-Mannerism in Italian Painting*. New York 1957.

Gaya Nuño, J.A. *Historia del arte español*. Madrid 1963.

Gudiol, J. *The Arts of Spain*. New York 1964.

Hagen, O. *Patterns and Principles of Spanish Art*. Madison (Wisconsin) 1948.

Hirmer, M. and P. de Palol *Early Medieval Art in Spain*. New York 1966.

Lafuente Ferrari, E. *Breve historia de la pintura española*. Madrid 1953.

La Souchère, E. de *An Explanation of Spain*. New York 1965.

Mayer, A.L. *Historia de la pintura española*. Madrid 1947.

Meléndez Pelayo, M. *Historia de las ideas estéticas en España*. 5 vols. Madrid 1964.

Menéndez Pidal, R. *Los españoles en la historia*. Madrid 1947.

Menéndez Pidal, R. *Los españoles en la literatura*. Madrid 1949.

O'Hara, F. *New Spanish Painting and Sculpture*. New York 1960.

Post, Ch.R. *A History of Spanish Painting*. 14 vols. Cambridge (Massachusetts) 1930–1966.

Smith, B. *Spain, A History in Art*. New York 1966.

Soria, M. and G. Kubler *Art and Architecture in Spain and Portugal and Their American Dominions, 1500–1800*. Harmondsworth 1959.

Index

(Page numbers in italics refer to illustrations on these pages)

STUDIO VISTA | DUTTON PICTUREBACKS
edited by David Herbert